11.99

A Selection of Books by Norman L. Geisler

Creating God in the Image of Man?
(Bethany House, 1997)

When Cultists Ask (Victor, 1997)

Love Is Always Right
(Thomas Nelson, 1996)

An Encyclopedia of Christian Evidences (Victor, 1996)

Roman Catholics and Evangelicals
(Baker, 1995)

In Defense of the Resurrection
(rev. by Witness Inc., 1993)

Answering Islam (Baker, 1993)

When Critics Ask (Victor, 1992)

Miracles and the Modern Mind
(Baker, 1992)

Matters of Life and Death
(Baker, 1991)

Thomas Aquinas: An Evangelical Appraisal (1991)

In Defense of the Resurrection
(Quest, 1991)

The Life and Death Debate
(Greenwood, 1990)

When Skeptics Ask (Victor, 1990)

Gambling: A Bad Bet
(Fleming H. Revell, 1990)

Come Let Us Reason (Baker, 1990)

Apologetics in the New Age
(Baker, 1990)

The Battle for the Resurrection
(Thomas Nelson, 1989)

The Infiltration of the New Age
(Tyndale, 1989)

Knowing the Truth About Creation
(Servant, 1989)

World's Apart (Baker, 1989)

Christian Ethics (Baker, 1989)

Signs and Wonders (Tyndale, 1988)

Philosophy of Religion (revised, 1988)

Origin Science (Baker, 1987)

Reincarnation Sensation
(Tyndale, 1986)

General Introduction to the Bible
(revised, Moody Press, 1986)

False Gods of Our Time
(Harvest House, 1985)

To Drink or Not to Drink
(Quest, 1984)

Explaining Hermeneutics
(ICBI, 1983)

Is Man the Measure? (Baker, 1983)

Miracles and Modern Thought
(Zondervan, 1982)

What Augustine Says (Baker, 1982)

Miracles and Modern Thought
(Zondervan, 1982)

What Augustine Says (Baker, 1982)

The Creator in the Courtroom—Scopes II (Baker, 1982)

Decide for Yourself (Zondervan, 1982)

Biblical Errancy (Zondervan, 1981)

Options in Contemporary Christian Ethics (Baker, 1981)

Introduction to Philosphy
(Baker, 1980)

Inerrancy (Zondervan, 1980)

To Understand the Bible, Look for Jesus (Baker, 1979)

The Roots of Evil (Zondervan, 1978)

A Popular Survey of the Old Testament (Baker, 1977)

Christian Apologetics (Baker, 1976)

From God to Us (Moody Press, 1974)

CREATING GOD IN THE IMAGE OF MAN?

DR. NORMAN L. GEISLER

BETHANY HOUSE PUBLISHERS
MINNEAPOLIS, MINNESOTA 55438

Published by Bethany House Publishers
A Ministry of Bethany Fellowship, Inc.
11300 Hampshire Avenue South
Minneapolis, Minnesota 55438

Printed in the United States of America.

Library of Congress Cataloging-in-Publication Data

Geisler, Norman L.
    Creating God in the image of man? : the new "open" view of God : neotheism's dangerous drift / Norman L. Geisler.
        p.   cm.
    Includes bibliographical references.
    ISBN 1–55661–935–9
    1. God—History of doctrines—20th century. 2. Evangelicalism—History—20th century. 3. Anthropomorphism—Controversial literature. 4. Theism—History—20th century. I. Title.
BT98.G44   1996
231'.044—dc21   96–45913
CIP

Acknowledgments

First of all, I wish to thank my faithful and dedicated wife for the laborious hours spent making this a better book. In addition, I wish to express appreciation for the able assistance of Steve Puryear, who helped significantly in researching this project. Most of all, I wish to thank the God of Abraham, Isaac, and Jacob, whose attributes are extolled in these pages, for His unchangeable love and unwavering faithfulness.

DR. NORMAN GEISLER is president of Southern Evangelical Seminary in Charlotte, North Carolina. The author of over 40 books, Dr. Geisler holds a B.A. and M.A. from Wheaton College, a Th.B. from William Tyndale College, and a Ph.D. from Loyola University in Chicago.

Contents

INTRODUCTION

The Bible declares that God made man in his own image (Genesis 1:26), but modern theology has returned the compliment. There are serious dangers in creating God in our image. This sort of thing is to be expected of unbelievers who turn from the living God and fashion a God after their own desires (cf. Romans 1:21f), but Christians should not tamper with the nature of the eternal God (1 Timothy 1:17). God is who he reveals himself to be, and not who we would like him to be.

This book warns of a dangerous trend within evangelical circles of creating God in man's image. As we shall show, this movement has significant practical implications for our faith. The view is called new theism or neotheism because it admittedly departs from the traditional view of God held by the Fathers of the church from the earliest times down to and through the Reformation and into contemporary evangelicalism. This venerable theistic tradition is now in danger of being lost, at least within an influential circle of Christian scholars.

In order to understand neotheism, it is first necessary to understand classical theism (chapter 2) and panentheism or process theology (chapter 3) from which neotheism so heavily borrows. Classical theism is best understood in terms of the other major worldviews with which it stands in contrast (chapter 1). Once both the biblical (chapter 4) and theological (chapter 5) charges against classical theism are examined, it remains only to scrutinize both the philosophical (chapter 6) and practical implications (chapter 7) of neotheism for the Christian life. Both chapter 7 and the appendices reveal consequences of neotheism regarding faith and devotion.

Our study yields a twofold conclusion: on the one hand, we conclude that neotheism is a significant deviation from the God of the Bible and from traditional Christian theology, which has dangerous consequences for the historic Christian faith; on the other hand, neotheism retains key elements of traditional theism, which warrant placing it within the broad spectrum of theism as opposed to panentheism (process theology).

Indeed, if neotheists were to consistently employ key beliefs like God's necessity, eternality, infinitude, creation *ex nihilo*, and supernatural intervention in the world, they would return to classical theism. It is our hope and prayer that this book will help nudge them in this direction.

One thing seems certain. If the logical consequences of neotheists' unorthodox beliefs about God are drawn out, they will be pushed more and more in the direction of process theology and the liberal beliefs entailed therein. Only time and logic will tell in which direction neotheism will go. Nonetheless, the distance from the orthodox view of God they have already traveled will have serious consequences for evangelicalism. This is true of any belief that creates God in man's image.

CHAPTER ONE

THE CHIEF COMPETITORS TO CHRISTIAN THEISM

A Buffet of Beliefs

This is a book about a new form of Christian theism called neotheism (new theism). In order to understand and evaluate this new version of theism, which is the purpose of this book, we must first understand the old theism. And, in turn, theism is best understood in contrast to the other worldviews that oppose it.

Worlds Apart

There are seven basic ways to understand the world or reality. They are theism, deism (theism minus miracles), finite godism (a limited god), pantheism (all is God), panentheism (all *in* God), polytheism (many gods), and atheism (no God or gods).

Many of the ancient Canaanites, Greeks, Egyptians, and Romans were polytheists. They worshiped a pantheon of gods. Of course various forms of theism (or monotheism) reacted against these, beginning with Judaism, Christianity, and then Islam. Eventually, however, theism degenerated into deism, finite godism, and even atheism.

Meanwhile, back in the East, pantheism continued to develop in Hinduism and certain forms of Buddhism. It also had roots in the late Greek neoplatonism of Plotinus (A.D. third century) and the modern rationalism of Spinoza (seventeenth century). Around the turn of the twentieth century, a new worldview emerged that is related to both theism and pantheism (all is God). This offered one more brand for the worldview shopper called panentheism (all *in* God). This view was fathered by Alfred North Whitehead in the first half of the twentieth century. It has been subsequently championed by many contemporary liberal thinkers, such as Charles Hartshorne, Schubert Ogden, and John Cobb.

Historically, theism was clearly distinct from all other worldviews. But, as we shall see (in chapter 3), with the exception of polytheism (many gods), which is compatible with pantheism, each worldview is logically exclusive of all the other worldviews. Spelling out their differences will help us understand the distinctives of theism, which in turn is the background for understanding neotheism—the topic of this book.

Seeing Through Different Glasses

People with different worldviews will often see the same facts in a very different way. For example, Christian theists view ultimate reality as a personal father, while many pantheists see it as an impersonal force. Orthodox Christians look at the empty tomb of Christ as evidence of a miracle. Deists and atheists search for a natural explanation to such questions as how Jesus could revive from his wounds and (if he died) who stole the body.

Theists (Jews, Christians, and Muslims) look at the fossil record and see in it evidence of creation. Naturalists (including atheists, pantheists, panentheists, and even present-day deists) see in it the proof of naturalistic evolution. A worldview does make a world of difference. Likewise, traditional theists expect to live only one mortal life, survive death, and then later be raised immortal in the same body in which they will have personal fellowship with a personal God forever. Non-theists do not. Most pantheists look for reincarnation into other mortal bodies until they burn up their karma and merge with an impersonal god. Atheists generally expect simply to die and become nonexistent.

Theism: An Infinite Personal God Exists Beyond and In the Universe

Theism is the worldview that affirms there is an infinite, eternal, personal God beyond the universe who created it, sustains it, and who can act within it in a supernatural way. Unlike atheism, theism insists that the physical universe is not all there is. And in contrast to pantheism, theism believes that God is not to be identified with all that is. The universe is not God, and God is not the universe. For a theist, God is as different from the universe he made as is a painter from his painting or a poet from his poem. The artist, like God, expresses himself in his work but also transcends it. That is, the Creator is more than his creation. Theism is represented by traditional Judaism, Christianity, and Islam.

Deism: God Is Beyond the Universe but Not In It

Deism grows out of theism. It is like theism minus the miracles. God made the world, but he does not involve himself with it in a direct way. Deism has also been called absentee godism. The deist's God is transcendent over the universe but not supernaturally active in it. Neither does the deistic God sustain the universe, as the God of theism does. Once created, the universe runs on its own. God tossed the world into existence and since that time it has moved on its own inertia. Like atheism, deism holds a naturalistic view of the world. The universe is void of, if not immune from, miracles. God made it but does not tinker with it. As the Master Watchmaker, God created the perfect watch that is not in need of continual intervention or repair. Deism is represented by men like Francois-Marie Voltaire, Thomas Jefferson, and Thomas Paine. Deistic views were also embraced by liberal forms of Christianity.

Finite Godism: A Finite Intelligent God Exists Beyond and In the Universe

In many ways modern finite godism is a reduced version of theism by way of deism. Each view progressively shrunk God. From the infinite personal God of theism who created the world, sustains it, and occasionally performs miracles in it, deism affirmed God's infinite power to create but rejected his ability to sustain or supernaturally intervene in the world. Finite godism further diminished the God of deism by admitting his creative power but denying it is infinite. God is beyond the universe and active in it but is limited in his nature and power.

Finite godism finds ancient roots in Plato and modern manifestations in John Stuart Mill, William James, Peter Bertocci, and more recently, Rabbi Harold Kushner, author of *When Bad Things Happen to Good People*[1] and *How Good Do We Have to Be?*[2]

Atheism: No God Exists In or Beyond the Universe

Atheism carries the diminution of God to the point of denial. It is the opposite of theism. It insists that the universe is all there is. It is the "whole show." Unlike pantheism, it denies that the universe is God. And in contrast to theism, atheism claims that no God exists anywhere, either in the universe or beyond it. The universe or cosmos is all there is or ever will be. Indeed, most atheists believe the universe (energy) is eternal. All atheists believe that the universe is self-sustaining. Some of the more famous atheists were Karl Marx, Friedrich Nietzsche, and Jean Paul Sartre.

Pantheism: God Is the Universe

Pantheists believe all is God, and God is all. They insist that the universe (reality) is all there is, and God cannot be more than all there is. For since God is infinite, there cannot be more than God. Hence, all that exists is part of God. Creator and creation are two different ways of viewing one reality. God is the universe (or, the all) and the universe is God. There is ultimately only one reality, not many different ones. Pantheism is represented by certain forms of Hinduism, Zen Buddhism, Christian Science, and many New Age religions.

Polytheism: There Are Many Gods Beyond the Universe and In It

Polytheism and pantheism are the only two worldviews that are compatible. As in Hinduism, it is possible to believe in one ultimate impersonal reality (like Brahman) and yet have many personal manifestations of this ultimate reality. Hinduism boasts millions of gods.

Since only the ultimate can be infinite (these can only be one "all"), each of these many gods must be finite, or limited.

There are, of course, many forms of polytheism that are not connected to pantheism. They affirm many finite gods beyond and in the physical universe. Unlike theism, polytheism believes in many gods. Likewise, they believe that deity is multiple, not singular. Often each one has his (or her) own sphere of operation. Sometimes there is a top god or one that is higher than the others (as Zeus was). This form of polytheism is labeled henotheism. In contrast to deism, the gods of polytheism are active in the world. The chief representatives of traditional polytheism are the Canaanite, Egyptian, Greek, and Roman deities. Two growing movements, modern Mormonism[3] and witchcraft, also embrace a plurality of gods.

Panentheism: God Is In the Universe

Panentheism (all *in* God, or God *in* all) should not be confused with pantheism (God *is* all), though there are similarities. According to panentheism, God is in the universe as a mind is in a body. The universe is God's "body." But there is another "pole" to God, namely, his eternal and infinite potential beyond the actual physical universe. Hence, the view is also called bipolar theism. Since God's "body" is in constant change, the name "process theology" is also given to this view.

In some respects panentheism is similar to theism. Both hold that there is one God and that he is more than the physical universe. However, there are also significant differences, because the panentheistic god is identified with the world in his "body" or physical pole. Further, unlike the God of theism, the panentheistic god does not create the world out of nothing (*ex nihilo*) but out of his own eternal resources (*ex Deo*). In this sense panentheism shares common ground with pantheism. Again, panentheism is represented by Alfred North Whitehead, Charles Hartshorne, Schubert Ogden, John Cobb, and Lewis Ford.

Neotheism: An Infinite Personal God Exists—With Limitations

The latest product in the worldview supermarket claims to be a "new and improved" version of theism in the direction of panentheism. Like theism it believes that God is the personal, infinite Creator of the universe out of nothing (*ex nihilo*). It also shares the belief that God can and does at times intervene in the world in a supernatural way. However, the god of neotheism lacks many of the traditional attributes of God, such as pure actuality (not potentiality), immutability (inability to change), simplicity (no parts or composition), and an infallible ability to foresee what future free agents may do. Neotheists believe that these are all "advantages" or "improvements" in the theistic view of God. Classical theists disagree. This conflict is the subject of the rest of this book.

What Difference Does It Make?

Worldviews make a world of difference in many ways. Let's take the three major worldviews to illustrate the point.

A Difference in Meaning

Because theism, atheism, and pantheism dominate the worldwide, worldview market, I will contrast them to demonstrate that their understanding of the crucial elements of a worldview differs significantly.

Let me comment here that some atheists, inconsistent with their own worldview, have adopted (from theism) a linear view of history. Karl Marx's belief in a future communistic utopia is a case in point. Likewise, B. F. Skinner's behavioral modification utopia in his *Walden Two*.

Each worldview has a different view of the origin, nature, and destiny of the world. Each has a differing concept of the origin, nature, and destiny of human beings. Likewise, the views differ as to the nature of truth and values, with only theism affirming that they are absolute.[4] Needless to say, these make a world of difference in how one thinks and acts. As one atheist, Jean Paul Sartre, put it: Without God, "nothing happens while you live. The scenery changes, people come in and go out, and that's all. There are no beginnings. Days are tacked on to days without rhyme or reason, an interminable, monotonous addition."[5]

WORLDVIEW	THEISM	PANTHEISM	ATHEISM
God	God made all	God is all	no god at all
world's origin	out of nothing	out of God	out of matter
world's nature	created spirit and matter	eternal spirit	eternal matter
God/world	God is beyond the world	God is the world	world only; no God
man's origin	creation	emanation	evolution
soul/body	soul & body	soul only	body only
after death	resurrection	reincarnation	annihilation
destiny of man	be with God	merge into God	annihilation
morality	absolute	relative	relative
truth	absolute	relative	relative
history	linear	cyclical	chaotic

A Difference in Values

There is a great gulf between different worldviews with regard to the nature of truth and values. For a theist certain things have ultimate value because God has so endowed them. Human life, for example, is sacred because God made it in his own image. This means that there are divine obligations to respect life and absolute prohibitions against murder. For an atheist, by contrast, life has only the value we give to it. This value is not sacred or divine; it is simply humanistic. It is not absolute but is merely relative. Often atheists are utilitarians, believing that an act is good if it brings good results and evil if it does not. A Christian believes that certain intended acts are either good or evil within themselves regardless of their results. So there is a radical difference in the value of the same act in these two systems.

A Final Word

It is not our purpose here to defend one major worldview over another. We have defended the theistic worldview in other places.

For a more popular treatment see *When Skeptics Ask*,[6] or for a more in-depth analysis, *Christian Apologetics*[7] should be consulted. The various worldviews are compared and contrasted in detail in *World's Apart*.[8]

The purpose of this chapter was to provide a broader focus within which the intramural debate between theism and neotheism can be better understood. We turn now to that task.

CHAPTER TWO

THE DISTINCTIVES OF CLASSICAL CHRISTIAN THEISM

Classical theism is the traditional Christian view of God—the God of Augustine, Anselm, Aquinas, the Reformers, the Puritans, and, until recently, the vast majority of evangelicals. This view was true of both classical Arminians and Calvinists. But now many contemporary evangelical Christian scholars believe that this view is in need of a serious overhaul. In order to understand the revision they desire to make in the traditional attributes of God, we must first look at precisely what Christian thinkers have long believed about God.

The Primary Origin

The primary origin of the new theism is classical theism. The secondary origin is rooted in panentheism (also called process theology).

The great medieval representatives of classical theism were St. Augustine, St. Anselm, and St. Thomas Aquinas. Protestant Reformers, Puritans, and most orthodox Catholics and Protestants also accept this view. Arguably, the greatest classical theist and the fountainhead of most theists after him was St. Thomas Aquinas (1224–1274). We will use his view to explain classical theism.

The Nature of the Theistic God

Classical theism is characterized by its belief in a personal, infinite, eternal, and immutable God who created the world out of nothing (*ex nihilo*) and who has supernaturally intervened in the world from time to time. God has absolute unity (oneness), simplicity (indivisibility), aseity (self-existence), pure actuality, and necessity (rather than contingency). God is both eternal (non-temporal) and infinite (without limits). God is also omnipotent (all-powerful) and omnipresent (everywhere present). God is also fully omniscient, knowing the future perfectly and infallibly, including what free creatures will do in the future.

God's Aseity (Self-Existence)

Most classical theists see God's aseity or pure self-existence as a key attribute. They cite the Bible in support of this position. This is true of the early church Fathers, as well as Augustine, Anselm, and Aquinas. In defending God's self-existence (aseity), classical theists like Aquinas are fond of quoting Exodus 3:14, where God said to Moses, "I am who I am." This they understand to refer to God as pure being or self-existence.

God is pure actuality with no potentiality in his being whatsoever. That is, God has no possibility of not existing. Whatever has potentiality (potency) needs to be actualized or affected by another. And since God is the ultimate Cause, there is nothing beyond him to actualize any potential he may have. Nor can God actualize his own potential to exist, since this would mean he caused his own existence. But a self-caused being is impossible, since it cannot create itself. Something has to exist before it can do anything. Even God cannot lift himself into being by his own ontological bootstraps. Thus, God must be pure actuality in his being.

Of course, God has the power or ability to create other things. But he cannot bring *himself* into being. He always was. But while God has the potential to *do* other things, he cannot *be* anything other than what he is. He has the power to *create* other things (active potency), but he does not have the potential (passive potency) to *exist* in any other way than he does, namely, as an infinite, eternal, necessary, and simple being.

God's aseity or pure actuality means that he *is* Being; everything else merely *has* being. God is pure actuality; all other things have both actuality and potentiality. Thus, God *cannot* not exist. All creatures *can* not exist. That is, they have the potentiality for nonexistence, whereas God does not. Only God is a necessary being. All other beings are contingent.

God's Simplicity (Indivisibility)

Since God is not composed in his being but is pure existence or pure actuality with no potentiality, it follows that he is simple and indivisible. A being that by nature is not composed cannot decompose. One that has no parts cannot be torn apart. Hence, God is absolute simplicity with no possibility of being divided. He is literally indivisible.

Likewise, God cannot be divided because to be divisible he would have the potentiality to be divided. But pure actuality has no potentiality in its being whatsoever. Hence, it must be absolutely simple or indivisible.

God's indivisibility follows also from his immutability (see following page). For if God could be divided, then he could change. But God is unchangeable by nature. Thus he cannot be divided. He must be absolutely simple in his nature.

God's Necessity (Non-contingency)

God is by nature an absolutely necessary being. If he exists, he must exist. He cannot *not* exist.

God is not a "may be" but a "must be" kind of being. He is not contingent, since he does not have the possibility not to exist. He is pure actuality and, as such, has no potentiality. But if he has no potentiality not to exist, then he must exist.

This is not to say that there must be a necessary being because the very idea demands one, as the ontological argument for God's existence claims. Most theists have considered and rejected Anselm's famous proof for God. It is only to say that if pure actuality (i.e., God) exists, then he must exist necessarily. But one cannot simply define it into existence; he must prove it. Aquinas offered his famous cosmological arguments for God's existence, which argue from some existing reality to its first cause.[1] And once we know, either from reason or revelation that God exists, then we can be sure that he must exist necessarily. For God is pure actuality with no potentiality in his being. But such a being has no potential not to exist. Hence, God must be a necessary being.

God's Immutability (Unchangeability)

In his epic *Summa Theologica*, Aquinas asks "whether God is altogether immutable."[2] He offers three basic arguments in favor of God's unchangeability. The first argument is based on the fact that a God of pure actuality ("I Am-ness") has no potentiality. For everything that changes has potentiality. But there can be no potentiality in God (he is pure actuality). It follows, therefore, that God cannot change.[3] Since God is actuality, as such, with no potentiality, we must conclude that he cannot change. For whatever changes must have the potential to change. But as pure actuality God has no potential to change. Therefore, God cannot change.

The second argument for God's immutability follows from his simplicity. Everything that changes is composed of what changes and what does not change. But there can be no composition in God (he is an absolutely simple being). Hence, God cannot change. An absolutely simple being has no composition. But whatever changes must be composed of what changes and what does not change. For if everything about a being changed, then it would not be the same being but an entirely new being. In fact, it would not be change but rather annihilation of one thing and a re-creation of something entirely new. Now if in every change something remains the same and something does not, then it must be composed of these two elements. But an absolutely simple being, such as God is, has no composition. Therefore, it follows that God cannot change.

The third argument for God's unchangeability argues from his absolute perfection. Briefly put, whatever changes acquires something new. But God cannot acquire anything new, since he is absolutely perfect; he could not be better. Therefore, God cannot change.

God is by his very nature an absolutely perfect being. If there were any perfection that he lacked, then he would not be God. However, to change one must gain something new. But to gain a new perfection is to have lacked it to begin with. Hence, God cannot change. If he did, he would not be God. Rather, he would be a being lacking in some perfection, not the absolutely perfect God that he is.

Aquinas also argues that God alone is immutable.[4] This is necessary because all creatures exist only because of the will of the Creator. It was his power that brought them into existence, and it is his power that keeps them in existence. Therefore, if he withdrew his power they would cease to exist. But whatever can cease to exist is not immutable. For ceasing to exist is a change, and an immutable being cannot change. Therefore, God alone is immutable; everything else could cease to exist.

God's Impassability (Without Passion)

Another classical attribute of God, one that comes under particular criticism from contemporary neotheists (see chapters 3–5), is impassability. God is without passion. For passion implies desire for what one does not have. But God, as an absolutely perfect being, has everything. He lacks nothing. For in order to lack something he would need to have a potentiality to possess it. But God is pure actuality, as we have said, with no potentiality whatsoever. Therefore, God has no passion for anything. He is completely and infinitely perfect in himself.

However, to say that God is impassable in the sense that he has no passions or cravings for fulfillment is not to say that he has no feeling. God feels anger at sin and rejoices in righteousness. But God's feelings are unchanging. He always, unchangingly, feels the same sense of anger at sin. And, likewise, he never ceases to rejoice in goodness and righteousness. Thus, God has no changing passions, but he does have unchanging feelings.

God's Eternity (Nontemporality)

According to classical theists, God is not temporal.[5] God is beyond time. Aquinas offers several arguments in support of this conclusion. One argument goes like this: whatever exists in time can be computed according to its befores and afters. However, a changeless being has no befores or afters; it is always the same. Consequently, God must be timeless.

Another argument for God's eternity also follows from immutability. It begins with the premise that whatever is immutable has no succession. In addition, whatever is in time has succession of one state after another. From this Aquinas concludes that whatever is immutable is not temporal. This argument stresses another aspect of time: whatever is temporal has successive states, one after the other. But as an immutable being, God has no changing states, one after another. Therefore, God cannot be temporal.

In brief, total immutability necessarily implies eternity.[6] For whatever changes substantially is in time and can be computed according to a before and an after. Whatever does not change cannot be in time, since it has no different states by which befores and afters can be computed; all are the same. It never changes. Therefore, whatever does not change is not temporal. Hence, God is eternal.

Not only is God eternal, but he alone is eternal.[7] The reason for this is that God alone is essentially immutable, since all creatures can cease to exist. But, as we have seen, eternity necessarily follows from immutability. It follows, then, that God alone is essentially eternal.

Aquinas distinguishes eternity from endless time[8] for several reasons. First of all, whatever is essentially whole is essentially different from what has parts. Eternity differs from time in this way (eternity is a now; time has now and then). Hence, eternity is essentially different from time.

In other words, God's eternity is not divided; it is all present to him in his one eternal now. So it must be essentially different from time, which comes only one moment after another.

Second, endless time is not eternity; it is just more of time. But eternity differs in kind (not just in degree) from time. That is, it differs essentially, not merely accidentally, from time. Endless time differs only accidentally from time because it is only an elongation of time. Thus, eternity is essentially different from endless time. Since endless time is simply time—just more of it—eternity must differ from it essentially. But more of the same thing is essentially the same thing. Therefore, endless time does not differ essentially from time.

Third, an eternal being cannot change, whereas time involves change by which the measurements of befores and afters can be made. Hence, an eternal being, such as God is, cannot change. In other words, whatever can be computed according to before and after is not eternal. Endless time can be computed according to befores and afters. Hence, endless time is not the same as eternity. The eternal is changeless, but what can be computed by its before and after has changed. It follows, then, that the eternal cannot be endless time. It must be something qualitatively different, not just different in quantity.

Fourth, Aquinas argues that there is a crucial difference in the "now" of time and the "now" of eternity.[9] The "now" of time is movable but the "now" of eternity is not. Therefore, the "now" of eternity is not the same as the "now" of time. The eternal "now" is unchanging, but the "now" of time is ever changing. Thus, they cannot be the same. There is only an analogy between time and eternity, not an identity. God's "now" has no past or future. But time's "nows," with the exception of the first moment, have a past and a future.

Some have mistakenly concluded that Aquinas does not believe in God's duration simply because he rejects temporality in God. Aquinas explicitly addressed this issue. He argued that duration occurs as long as actuality exists. But things endure in different ways. Eternity (God) endures without any potency. Aeviternity (angels) endure with completely actualized potency. And time (man) endures with progressive actualized potency. It follows, therefore, that the essential difference comes from the condition of the actuality that is measured.

God is act (actuality) as such, unmeasured by any potentiality. Angels are act as received in pure forms that wholly receive their actuality from creation. Man is act as received in form/matter (soul/body) that progressively receives his actuality. In brief, God actually endures, but he endures as pure actuality. Since he has no potentiality, he cannot endure progressively. He endures in a much higher way—as pure actuality.

Another way to understand the difference between God's eternity and time is to recognize that time is an accidental change, not a substantial change. A substantial change is a change in what something *is*; an accidental change is a change in what something *has*. Aquinas points out that time is an accidental change. And only man, not God or angels, has accidental change. So, only man is in time. Angels undergo substantial change (creation), but this does not involve time. The only mode of being that existed before angels began was an eternal mode (God).

A substantial change for man is a change into or out of time but not a change in time. But God cannot change substantially or accidentally. Since he is a necessary being he cannot go out of existence. And since he is a simple being he has no accidents. Therefore, God cannot be temporal in any way, since all time involves change.

God's Unity (Oneness)

Aquinas offers three reasons for God's unity.[10] The first argument is taken from the simplicity of God. Whatever is an absolutely simple being cannot be more than one. Moreover, God is an absolutely simple being. Therefore, God cannot be more than one being. A simple being cannot be more than one, since to be more than one there must be parts, but simple beings have no parts. Absolutely simple beings are not divisible. Therefore, they cannot be more than one.

Secondly, God's perfection argues for his unity. For, if two or more Gods existed they would have to differ. And in order to differ one must have what the other one lacks. But an absolutely perfect being cannot lack anything. Therefore, there can only be one absolutely perfect being.

Thirdly, God's unity can be inferred from the unity of the world. The world is composed of diverse things. Diverse things do not come together unless they are ordered. But the world has an ordered unity. Therefore, there must be one Orderer of the world. He also asserts that essential unity is better explained by one Orderer than by many orderers. For one is the essential cause of oneness, but many is only the accidental cause of oneness. Therefore, it is reasonable to infer that there is only one cause of the world, not many. In short, this is a universe, and a universe calls for a unitary cause (namely, one).

The Unchangeable Relationship of the World to a Theistic God

If God is unchanging in his being, then it is natural to inquire how he can relate to a changing world. For it would appear that if the changing world is related to God, then God must somehow be tainted by his association with it. Aquinas anticipated this kind of objection and argued that there is a real relationship between the unchanging world and the unchanging God.[11] He observed that there are three kinds of relations: one where both terms are ideas (e.g., the same is the same as itself); another where both terms are real (e.g., a small thing compared to a large thing); and one where one is real and one is an idea (e.g., on the right side).

Now since creatures are truly dependent on God but God is not truly dependent on them, they are related as real to an idea. That is, God *knows* about the relationship of dependence but he does not *have* it. Thus, when there is a change in the creature there is no change in God. Just as when the man changes his position from one side of the pillar to the other, the pillar does not change; only the man changes in relation to the pillar. So, while the relationship between God and creatures is real, God is in no sense dependent on that relationship.

It is important to note that Aquinas is only denying *dependent* relationships, not all *real* ones. He is denying that God changes in his relationship with the world but not that there are real changes in the world's relation with God. The man's relation to the pillar changes when he moves, but the pillar does not change.

The real relation of God to the world is made even more clear when Aquinas treats the question of how the temporal world is related to the eternal God.[12] He argues that temporal relations exist only in God's ideas of temporal things but not in reality. For example, to create is a temporal relation. But God is not a creature. Hence, to have a relationship with the temporal world God does not have to be temporal. *It makes no more sense to say God has to be temporal in order to relate to a temporal world than to say he has to be a creature in order to create.*

God is related to creatures because he is their Creator. And creatures are related to God because he is their Creator. The real relation of dependence, then, is in the creature, not in the Creator. Therefore, the relation of God to creatures is real and not merely ideal. However, it is a real relationship of dependence on the part of the creatures but not a relation of dependence on the part of God.[13]

The Infinite Unchangeable Knowledge of the Theistic God

There are many aspects of God's unchangeable knowledge. Several are worthy of note in this connection.

God Knows Himself Simply

If God is absolutely simple, then how can he know himself? All knowledge involves both a knower and a known. But God has no such duality, being completely simple. Aquinas argues that all knowing involves a knower and a known. But in self-knowledge the knower and known are identical. Hence, God can only know himself through himself.[14] In short, God knows himself by himself and in himself. And since God is simple, it follows that he knows himself simply.

God Knows Himself Perfectly

Furthermore, God also knows himself perfectly. Something is known perfectly when its potential to be known is completely realized. And there is no unactualized potentiality in God, since he has no potentiality whatsoever. God is complete actuality, or pure actuality. Therefore, God knows himself perfectly. His self-knowledge is completely actualized, that is, it is complete actuality.[15]

God's Knowledge Is Identical to His Essence

God's knowledge is identical with his essence. For if God's acts of knowledge were distinct from his essence, then they would be related as actuality to potentiality. But there can be no potentiality in God; he is pure actuality. Therefore, God's knowledge and essence are identical.[17] This does not mean that God cannot know things other than himself. For God is the efficient cause of all things. And all effects preexist in their efficient causes. Hence, whatever exists must preexist in God who is its efficient cause. And God knows himself perfectly. But to know himself perfectly entails knowing all of the various kinds of perfection in himself as well as those that can participate in his likeness. Therefore, it follows that God knows whatever exists perfectly insofar as they all preexist in him.[18] In short, God is omniscient or all-knowing. As we shall see, this total omniscience is denied by neotheism (see chapters 4, 5).

God Knows Evil Only Indirectly

Just because God knows perfectly does not mean that he cannot know evil. For perfect knowledge of things must include knowing all that can occur to them. And evil can occur to good things (as a corruption of them). Hence, God can know evil. But things are knowable only in the way in which they are (exist). And evil exists only as a privation in good things (but not in itself). Therefore, God knows evil as a privation in a good thing but does not know evil in itself. He knows it the way darkness is known by light but not in itself.[16]

God Knows Changing Things

Since God is unchanging and his knowledge is identical with his essence, does this mean that God cannot know changing things? Not at all. For God knows everything in one eternal now, including the past, present, and future. And God knows the future before it happens in time, since he knows it in himself as its cause. Therefore, when time changes, God's knowledge does not change, since he knew it eternally in himself. In other words, God knows *what* we know but not in the *way* we know it, that is, in successive time frames. God knows the whole of time from (in) eternity.[19] So God knows changing things but not in a changing way.

God Knows Many Things

Likewise, God is one but he knows many things. For God knows his own essence perfectly. And knowing his essence perfectly entails knowing it according to every mode by which it can be known, namely, in itself and as participated in by creatures. But every creature has its own proper form in which it is like God. It follows, therefore, that God knows the form or idea of every creature as it is modeled after him.

God Knows Singular Things

In brief, the *basis* for what God knows is his own essence, but the *extent* of what he knows is not limited to that one essence but reaches to all things like it.[20] God's knowledge of all things in himself does not mean that he only knows other things in general but not in particular. For God's knowledge extends as far as his causality. And God's causality extends to singular things, since he is the cause of every individual thing. Therefore, God knows singular things.[21]

God Knows All Things Perfectly

Furthermore, God has a perfect knowledge of everything. He is omniscient (all-knowing). And to know something only in general but not in particular is improper knowledge. So, God knows everything properly. That is, he does not know the radius of a circle merely by knowing the center; he knows the radii as well as the center. This is further demonstrated by the fact that perfect knowledge involves the ability to distinguish one thing from another. That is, he knows not only what things have in common (existence) but how they differ (essence). Therefore, God knows all things in their individual essences. But all things preexist in God's knowledge. Therefore, all things preexist in God's knowledge not only with regard to their existence but also with regard to their individual essences. In addition, by knowing himself perfectly, God knows perfectly all the different ways his perfection can be shared by others. For there is within the essence of God all the knowledge of all possible kinds of things that his will could actualize. Hence, God knows all the particular things that could ever be actualized.[22]

God Knows Intuitively

God knows the *same things* we do, but he does not know them the *same way* we know them. Our knowledge is discursive or inferential, moving from premises to conclusions. In human knowledge there is twofold discursiveness: where one thing is known *after* another, and where one thing is known *through* another. But God cannot know things sequentially, since he is timeless and knows all things eternally at once. Nor can God know things inferentially, for he is simple and knows all things through the oneness of himself. Therefore, God cannot know anything discursively, inasmuch as discursive knowledge implies a limitation on the part of the knower.[23]

Furthermore, even though God knows *other* things than himself, nonetheless, he knows them *in and through* himself. For God does not know other things through himself either successively or inferentially but simultaneously and intuitively. In brief, God knows the created effects *in* himself intuitively but not through himself in a discursive way.[24] This is not an imperfection in God's knowledge but a perfection. For God's knowledge is more perfect precisely because he does not have to know things discursively or sequentially through their causes but knows them directly and intuitively.[25]

God Knows the Future Perfectly and Completely

God not only knows all things in and through himself, but he also causes all things by his knowledge. For God causes all things by his being. And God's being and his knowledge are identical. Hence, God causes all things by his knowledge.[26] This does not mean that creation is eternal because he is eternal. For God causes all things as they are in his knowledge. But that creation should be eternal was not in God's knowledge (this Aquinas accepts by faith in the authority of Scripture). So, even though God's knowledge is eternal, creation is not eternal.[27] Neither does this mean that humans are not free, for God as the primary cause uses the secondary cause of free choice to accomplish his ends. Man is truly free and God knows exactly how that freedom will be exercised.

God's knowledge is not simply of the actual; he also knows the potential. He knows both what is and what could be. For God can know whatever is real in any way it can be known. Now both the actual and the potential are real. Only the impossible has no reality. Thus, whatever is potential is real. This being the case, it follows that God can know what is potential as well as what is actual.[28] This means that God can know future contingents, that is, things that are dependent on free choice. For the future is a potential that preexists in God.

And God knows whatever exists in himself as the cause of those things.[29]

Furthermore, since God is a timeless being, he knows all of time in one eternal moment. But the future is part of time. Therefore, God knows the future, including the free acts to be performed in it. Of course, whatever God knows is known infallibly, since God cannot err in his knowledge. And since God knows future contingents, it follows that they too are known infallibly by God. They are contingent with regard to their immediate cause (human free choice) but necessary with regard to God's knowledge. God can do this without eliminating free choice, for an omniscient being can know whatever is not impossible to know. And it is not impossible for a timeless being to know a necessary end that is caused by a contingent means.

In brief, God can know a "must be" through a "may be" but not a "can't be." Therefore, an omniscient being (God) knows all future contingents as necessarily true. This he can do because God knows necessarily that what will be must be. That is, if it will be and God knows it, then what God knows about what will be must be true. An omniscient mind cannot be wrong about what it knows. Therefore the statement "Everything known by God must necessarily be" is true if it refers to the statement of the truth of God's knowledge, but it is false if it refers to the necessity of the contingent events.[30] This view of God's foreknowledge and free will is compatible with both classical Arminianism and moderate Calvinism.[31]

The Unchangeable Will of the Theistic God

According to classical theism, God cannot change his will. For his will must act in accord with his unchangeable nature. And as was shown above, God's nature cannot change.

Furthermore, God is omniscient, and an omniscient being knows everything. But whoever knows everything cannot learn anything, since he already knows everything there is to know. Hence, there is no reason for God to change his mind, since he knows eternally every condition that will come to pass. So there is never anything new that he would have to take into consideration in making a decision.

As Aquinas argued, just like God's knowledge, his will is also unchanging. Having a will does not mean that God must change. For God is the object of his will, namely, his divine goodness. And whatever is in one's self necessitates no movement outside one's self to attain. Hence, God does not have to move outside himself to attain his own proper end. That is, God's essence is his own end; there is no end outside of God. And the will is an inclination toward one's own end. So, there is a will in God inasmuch as he inclines toward his own good.

Furthermore, the will also involves love and delight in what is possessed. But God loves and delights in the possession of his own nature. Therefore, God has will in the sense of delight but not in the sense of desire.[32]

Simply because God wills things only in himself does not mean that he wills only himself. For it is in accord with the nature of being to communicate its good to others. And God is being par excellence; he is the source of all being. Hence, it is in accord with the nature of God to will beings other than himself.[33] So God wills things other than himself in and through himself. God is not other than himself, but he can will things other than himself in himself. For will implies a relationship. Hence, although God is not other than himself, he wills things other than himself.[34] Just as God understands other things through himself, so God wills other things through himself.

God Cannot Be Moved to Change by Another

Contrary to the claim of neotheists, classical theists insist that nothing can move God to change his will. For what is moved by itself to act is not moved by another. Hence, God is not moved by another when he wills to create through himself.[35] But in willing things other than himself, God is not moved by any insufficiency in himself but rather by the sufficiency in himself, that is, by his own goodness. Therefore, willing other things through his own sufficiency denotes no insufficiency in God.[36] Just as God knows many things (truth) through the oneness of his essence, so he can will many things through the oneness (good) of his will.[37]

As to whether our prayer moves God to change his mind, classical theists insist that God knew in advance whether we would pray and took our prayer into consideration in ordaining the answer. Nothing catches an omniscient being by surprise. God ordains prayer as a means by which he accomplishes his will. God is "moved" by our prayers in the sense that he feels our needs and passions and has predetermined that they will be utilized in accomplishing his ultimate purposes. But to affirm that something new is brought to God in our prayers that causes him to change his mind is to claim that God did not really know everything from the beginning. This contradicts the words of Scripture that he makes known the end from the beginning (Isaiah 46:10).

God Wills Things in Two Ways

God is a necessary being and what he wills, he does so with necessity. But there are two ways God wills things with necessity, namely with *absolute* necessity—his own goodness. This God must will; he cannot choose otherwise. Or, God can will with *conditional* necessity, such as willing the goodness of creatures. This God need not will, but if he does will it, he cannot thereby not will it. But he does not have to will it to begin with. Now whatever is willed by conditional necessity is not absolutely necessary. Creation is willed by conditional necessity.

Therefore, it was not necessary that God create anything. Of course, God wills other things *because of* his own goodness but not as *necessitated by* it. For God can exist without willing other things. God need only will his own goodness necessarily and other things contingently. Therefore, these other things need not be willed with absolute necessity. Of course, it is necessary to God's will that he will his own nature necessarily. But it is not necessary to God's will that he will created goods necessarily. Hence, it is not necessary that God wills anything other than himself. But God did will things other than himself. Thus, God must have willed these other things voluntarily.[38]

God's Unchangeable Will and Free Choice

If God must will things necessarily it would seem to leave no room for free choice. But this is not the case. It is true that as a necessary being he must know necessarily whatever he knows. But it does not follow that he must necessarily (i.e., not freely) will what he wills. Aquinas notes that divine knowing is necessarily related to the created thing known, because knowledge exists in the knower (God), which is one with his essence. But divine willing is not necessarily related to the created thing willed, since willing is of the things as they exist in themselves outside of the necessity of the divine essence. Hence, God knows necessarily what he knows but does not will necessarily what he wills.

Further, all things exist necessarily in God, but nothing exists necessarily outside him. But God need only will what is necessarily of his own nature. Therefore, God need only will other things as they exist in him but not as they exist in themselves outside of himself.[39]

God's will is the cause of all things. For all created effects preexist in God according to his nature. God's knowledge is identical with his nature. Hence, all created things preexist in God's knowledge. Now will is the inclination to act on what one knows. Therefore, all created effects flow from God's will.[40] Of course, God must bestow good on all he chooses to create; God cannot create evil. But it is not necessary that God will any being or good other than himself. Therefore, God need only bestow good on what he chooses to create.[41]

God's Will Is Never Caused by Another

As to whether God's will is ever caused by anything else, Aquinas gives a negative answer. God's will *is* the cause of all things, and what is the Cause of all needs no cause at all. For in God the means and the end preexist in the cause as willed together. Hence, the end willed is not the cause of God's willing; rather his willing is the cause of the end (and means) willed. And since all things preexist in the first cause (God's will), then there is no cause for God's will. For God's will is the first cause and there is no cause of the first cause; rather, the first cause is the cause of everything else.[42]

God's Will Can Never Fail

Neither can God's will ever fail. For the will of God is the universal cause of all things. Therefore, the will of God never fails but is always fulfilled, for what falls from God's will in one order returns to God's will in another order, e.g., what falls from the order of his favor returns to the order of his justice. Particular effects may fall short of particular forms but not of their universal form. For example, something may fail to be a man or an animal, but it can't fail to be a being. But the failure of a particular cause is included within the success of the universal cause. So, when particular causes fail, the universal cause does not fail. God cannot fail.[43]

Aquinas distinguishes, however, between the *antecedent* and *consequent* will of God, not with regard to his will in itself but regarding the thing willed. God wills antecedently that all should be saved.[44] But God wills consequently that some will be lost, namely, those whom justice demands. But what is willed antecedently is not willed absolutely but only conditionally. Only the consequent is willed absolutely in view of all the circumstances.

God wills some things through secondary causes, such as free choice. And first causes are sometimes hindered through defects in secondary causes. For instance, the locomotion of the body is hindered through a bad leg. Likewise, God's antecedent will is sometimes hindered by a defect in a secondary cause. But his consequent will is never frustrated. For first universal causes cannot be hindered by defective secondary causes, any more than goodness as such can be hindered by evil. And God is the universal first cause of being. Therefore, God's will cannot be hindered in his causing of being.[45]

God's Will Can Never Be Changed

Nothing can change the will of God. For he is omniscient, and so what he knows will be, will be. God's will is in perfect accord with his knowledge. Therefore, God's will is unchangeable. This does not mean that God does not will that some things change. It means that God's will does not change, even though he does will that other things change.[46] Of course, the Bible speaks of God repenting, etc., but God repents only in a metaphorical sense, as man views it. Actually, God knew from eternity who would repent. And God's will includes intermediate causes such as human free choice. So God knows what the intermediate causes will choose to do. And God's will is in accord with his unchangeable knowledge. Therefore, God's will never changes, since he wills what he knows will happen. That is to say, what is willed by conditional necessity does not violate human freedom, since what is willed is conditioned on their freely choosing it. God wills the salvation of men only conditionally. Therefore, God's will to salvation does not violate human free choice; it utilizes it. Both classical Arminians and moderate Calvinists agree. Among evangelicals, only extreme Calvinists demur.

Summing It All Up

Classical theism is the soil out of which neotheism grows and against which it reacts. In common with neotheism, classical theism believes that God is the infinite, necessary, uncaused, omnipotent (all-powerful) Creator of the universe out of nothing (*ex nihilo*). On the other hand, neotheists disagree with classical theism's belief in a simple, immutable, nontemporal, purely actual, and fully omniscient (all-knowing) God. It is these differences, their coherence and consequences, that will occupy most of the rest of this book (chapters 4–7). But first we must examine the source from which these differences spring, namely, contemporary process theology (panentheism).

CHAPTER THREE

REMAKING GOD IN OUR IMAGE

While neotheism (new theism) is a descendent of classical theism (see chapter 2), nevertheless, it has undergone some serious mutations in the direction of panentheism (all in God) or process theology. Or, to borrow a similar figure, conscious crossbreeding of young theists and panentheists have produced a new species—neotheists. Thus, in order to understand neotheism properly we must take a careful look at the other side of its parentage.

Panentheism means all in God. It too is the result of a mixed marriage between theism (God created all) and pantheism (all is God). Panentheism also bears other names such as process theology (since it views God as a changing being), bipolar theism (since it believes God has two poles), and organicism (since God is viewed as a gigantic organism).

Theism vs. Panentheism

A contrast between classical theism (see chapter 2) and panentheism will help focus the distinctives. The following chart summarizes these differences.

TWO VIEWS IN CONTRAST

	THEISM	PANENTHEISM
G	Creator of the world	Director of the world process
O	(creation is *ex nihilo*)	(creation is *ex Deo*)
D	sovereign over the world	working with the world
	independent of the world	mutually dependent on the world
I	unchanging being	changing being (=becoming)
S	absolutely perfect	growing in perfection
	monopolar (one pole)	bipolar (two poles)
	actually infinite	actually finite

Rather than viewing God as the infinite, unchanging sovereign Creator of the world who brought it into existence, panentheists think of God as a finite, changing, Director of world affairs who works in cooperation with the world in order to achieve greater perfection in his nature.

By contrast, theism thinks of God's relation to the world as a painter to a painting. The painter exists independently of the painting; he brought the painting into existence, and yet his mind is expressed in the painting. Panentheism sees God's relation to the world the way a mind is related to a body. In fact, it views the world as God's "body" (one pole) and his "mind" as the other pole. However, like some modern thinkers who believe the mind is dependent on the brain, panentheists believe God is dependent on the world. Yet there is a sense in which the world is dependent on God. There is, in fact, a mutual dependence. As Schubert Ogden put it, since the world is God's body, it is "necessarily dependent on a world of other beings."[1] God does not need any particular world, only some world or other. And whatever world exists, God and that world are interdependent. The world needs God to give it ultimate significance, and God needs the world so that he may retain the value actualized by his self-creative creatures and thus ever reach toward a more fulfilled cosmic experience.[2]

Explaining the Panentheistic Model of God

While panentheism is a modern view of God, it has roots in ancient Greece. Many Greek philosophers were forerunners of today's panentheists. Several are worthy of note.

The roots of panentheism. Plato's *Demiurgos* (world Former) bears some similarities to panentheism. While Plato's cosmos was not really a part of God, nonetheless his god was finite and struggled with the chaos to form it into the cosmos. This provides the dualistic background for what became two "poles" in God. Even before this, Heraclitus's (c. 500 B.C.) philosophy that everything is in flux is a forerunner of the process idea, in that he asserted the world is a constantly changing process. Nonetheless, it has an unchanging Logos beneath it.

In the modern world, G. W. F. Hegel (d. 1831) posited a God who progressively unfolded in the world process. This was another significant step toward panentheism. In addition to this there is the cosmic evolutionism of Herbert Spencer (d. 1903), in which the whole universe is viewed as an unfolding and developing process. Immediately following this, Henri Bergson proposed a *Creative Evolution* (1907) of a "life force" (*elan vital*) which drives evolution forward in "leaps." Later he identified this force with God (1935). Earlier, Samuel Alexander's *Space, Time, and Deity* (1920) pioneered a process view of God's relation to the temporal universe.

While there are several roots to panentheism, the main trunk is Alfred North Whitehead, great English mathematician and son of an Anglican minister. His major books on the topic include: *Religion in the Making* (1926), *Process and Reality* (1929), *Adventures of Ideas* (1933), and *Modes of Thought* (1938). Whitehead's most noted student during his Harvard tenure was Charles Hartshorne. Hartshorne produced a number of books on the topic, including: *A Natural Theology for Our Time, Man's Vision of God, Creative Synthesis and Philosophic Method,* and *The Logic of Perfection.* One of Hartshorne's noted protégés was Schubert M. Ogden, who wrote several works on panentheism, including *Toward a New Theism, In Process Philosophy and Christian Thought, The Reality of God, Faith and Freedom,* and *Theology in Crisis.* In addition, there is Lewis Ford, who produced *The Lure of God,* stressing God's role as Cosmic Enticer who never overpowers free creatures but merely woos them to embrace his overall purpose.

The Attributes of the Panentheistic God

Unlike the God of classical theism (see chapter 2), who is pure Actuality, the panentheistic God has two poles—an actual pole and a potential pole. He is bipolar as opposed to monopolar. These two poles possess contrasting attributes, such as necessary-contingent, infinite-finite, and eternal-temporal.

God is bipolar. All panentheists agree that God has two poles: an actual pole (the world) and a potential pole (beyond the world). All hold that God is changing, finite, and temporal in his actual pole. And all affirm that his potential pole is unchanging and eternal. The major difference in how they view God is whether God in his actual pole is one actual entity (event) or a society of actual entities. Alfred North Whitehead holds the former view, and Charles Hartshorne holds the latter. Some panentheists, such as John Cobb, reject the disjunction between the two poles in God. He claims that God acts as a unity, not simply in one pole or the other.

These two "natures" are related as potential to actual. In the left column is *what God can be*. In the right column is *what God actually is* at any given moment in the ongoing process of the world. The former is called God's "primordial nature" and the latter his "consequent nature."

PANENTHEISTIC GOD:
TWO POLES

Primordial nature	Consequent nature
God's "mind"	God's "body"
God's vision	God's achievement
Potential pole	Actual pole
Unconscious drive	Conscious realization
Conceptual	Physical
Abstract	Concrete
Beyond the world	The actual world
Eternal	Temporal
Absolute	Relative
Unchanging	Changing
Imperishable	Perishable
Unlimited	Limited
Necessary	Contingent
Eternal objects	Actual entities

Hartshorne noted that in their concreteness God and the world are one. It is in this sense that Hartshorne says "God is the wholeness of the world."[3] There is more to God than the world (his consequent pole); God also has a primordial pole that is beyond the world. However, this does not mean that God is identical to the world as in pantheism. God literally permeates the world in his concrete pole but without destroying the individuality of his creatures. God accomplishes this by including within himself the "totality of all ordinary causes and effects" without becoming identical to them. Thus the world is in God, but he is distinguishable, though not separable, from the world.[4]

An analogy Hartshorne is fond of using to explain God's relation to the world is the mind-body analogy. He maintains that the human body "is really a 'world' of individuals, and a mind . . . is to that body something like an indwelling God."[5] Applied to God, Hartshorne thinks this analogy yields the following conclusions concerning God's relation to the world. God is related to the world as the human mind is related to the human body. Like humans, God has direct control over his world-body. In a similar way God influences the living members of his cosmic body, and they influence him. The dissimilarity between the human mind-body relationship and the divine mind-body relationship is that God's awareness of what occurs in his world-body is always vivid and distinct and all-encompassing. On the other hand, a human being's awareness of what occurs in his own body is generally indistinct and always partial or fragmentary.[6] Since the world is God's "body," its actual makeup is crucial, then, to understanding the actual nature of God. There are several characteristics of the world.

The world is pluralistic. That is to say, it is made up of many "actual entities," which Whitehead defines as "final facts," "drops of experience," or "actual occasions." In other words, the world is an atomistic series of events. "Actuality is incurably atomic."[7] Hence, God is not an absolutely simple being as classical theism asserts. Rather, he is posited as a highly complex being, both in his potential nature and in his actual nature.

The world is in process. Change is fundamental to the actual nature of God. "The ancient doctrine that 'no one crosses the same river twice' is extended. No thinker thinks twice; and, to put the matter more generally, no subject experiences twice." There are no unchanging beings. "The simple notion of an enduring substance, either essentially or accidentally . . . proves itself mistaken."[8] There is no concrete being; all is becoming. "It belongs to the nature of every 'being' that it is a potential for every becoming." "There is a becoming of continuity, but no continuity of becoming." Whitehead's student Charles Hartshorne maintains that "becoming is not a special mode of reality, rather it is its overall character." In fact, "becoming is reality itself." And since the past has already become and the future has not yet become, only the present moment can become (that is, be in the process of being created). Consequently, when he speaks of reality he means "as of now."[9] In "human experiences" these nows "normally" occur "some 10–20 per second." Applied on a cosmic scale, this means that every being that exists, especially God, is in great flux, being created anew each moment. With every new event there are new atoms, new cells, new plants, new animals, new people—even a new God. Hartshorne holds that a new event means a new God, just as a man is a new man every moment.[10]

The world is ordered. Despite the atomic distinctness and continual change in the universe, there is order. This order is given by God. In his primordial nature God gives order to all eternal objects (forms) and the 'consequent nature' of "God is the physical prehension by God of the actualities of the evolving universe."[11] In fact, God is the order of the actual world. He not only gives it order, he constitutes that order himself. This is Whitehead's equivalent to the "teleological argument" for God's existence. That is, it is similar to the argument that design in the world implies a Designer of the world, except that in panentheism God and the world are not two different beings.

God is personal. Unlike many pantheists, proponents of panentheism affirm that God is personal. But, contrary to Whitehead, Hartshorne does not take God to be an actual entity. Rather, he understands God to be "an enduring society of actual entities."[12] But unlike other societies, God endures no matter what world exists and regardless of the circumstances in any given world. Further, the divine society includes all non-divine societies.[13] Like other individuals, God is partially new each moment. Hence God in his present concrete state is not identical to himself in his previous concrete states. The God one may serve now is not the God one may have served yesterday, or the one he may serve tomorrow.[14]

God is only relatively perfect. Unlike classical theism, the God of process theology is not absolutely perfect. He is only relatively perfect.

According to Hartshorne, perfection means that "God cannot conceivably be surpassed or equaled by any other individual, but he can surpass himself, and thus his actual state is not the greatest possible state."[15] In short, God "is the being unsurpassable *by another.*"[16] He has no possible rival to himself. And he is perpetually surpassing himself at every moment, actualizing more and more potentialities, enriching himself with more value, forever reaching toward a more complete perfection, which can never be fully realized.[17] In Hartshorne's words, "only God can surpass God, but this he perpetually does by ideally absorbing the riches of creation into himself."[18]

God is actually finite. According to Hartshorne, God is finite (limited). He is only potentially infinite, but actually finite, both in power and perfection. That is, "God is infinite in what he could be, not in what he is; he is infinitely capable of actuality rather than infinitely actual." In fact, God could not be infinitely actual, for to become infinitely actual God would have to actualize all possibility, which is actually impossible since "possibility is in principle inexhaustible."[19]

God is actually finite. For all that God could be is never actualized at any given moment or stretch of time. God must express himself in and relate himself to a finite, changing world, which is his physical pole. And because there is a finite number of finite beings at any one time, God can only interact finitely. Moreover, God's creatures further "limit" his activity by some of their actions—namely by "unlucky or even perverse actions." This is so because God's realization of any potential is dependent upon his creature's actions. Thus they may frustrate his realization of value, and, at any rate, some creatures must exist for God to realize any value at all.[20]

God is temporal. God is also a temporal being, subject to the successions of time. He is eternal only in the sense that in his concrete pole there is "an actually infinite regress of past stages." God has been in process through "an infinite series of actual worlds, or world states," which have been "successive to one another."[21] In this sense, God is eternal or endless. But he does not transcend time. He is, in fact, *in* time. Panentheists flatly reject the claim of traditional theism (see chapter 2) that God is eternal in a non-temporal sense.

God is spatial. God is in space as well as in time. God is all-spatial, for the space-time world is his "body." This is another one of God's limitations. His actual nature is co-extensive with the space-time world. Thus, process theology rejects the traditional attribute of the immensity (non-spatialness) of God, just as it rejects God's eternity (non-temporality).

God is limited in knowledge. Unlike classical theism, panentheism rejects God's omniscience. Since God knows contingent, changing beings, his knowledge of them is also contingent and changing. This is because the knower, whoever it may be, is always dependent on and thus relativized by the known. Hence, since God knows every existent thing, he is related to and relativized by every existent thing. In this respect, God is said to be supremely relative. But "regardless of circumstances, of what happens anywhere or when, God will enjoy unrestricted cognitive relativity to all that coexists with him."[22] In this sense, God is absolute—he is the absolutely relative One.

God is supreme love. Divine love is the attribute that Hartshorne believes comprehensively sums up the idea of God. Love is the "realization in oneself of the desires and experiences of others, so that one who loves can inflict suffering only insofar as he undergoes this suffering himself, willingly and fully."[23] Human beings love inadequately, for they cannot fully know and thus enter into another's experiences and desires. God, however, can adequately love all, for he feels all desires for what they are and experiences all experiences as they are.[24] Only he "unwaveringly understands and tries to help" his creatures, and only he "takes unto himself the varying joys and sorrows of all others," and only his happiness is eminently capable of alteration as a consequence.[25] And because God loves all fully, yet eminently cares about all differences, and eminently and sympathetically responds to them accordingly, he is the perfect lover.[26]

The Nature of Creation

For panentheists, God is not the Creator of the world; he is only Director of world progress. God did not bring the world into existence, he merely guides its progress. Since the universe is eternal, God has been forming it from eternity. God "does not create eternal objects, for his nature requires them in the same degree that they require him." Thus, God is not *before* all creation, but *with* all creation. He does not bring the universe into existence, he merely directs its ongoing progress. Creation from nothing (as theism affirms) is too coercive. Hence, the temptation to interpret God's creative power by means of coercive power is extremely great. "If the entire created order is dependent for its existence upon his will, then it must be subject to his full control. . . . Insofar as God controls the world, he is responsible for evil: directly in terms of the natural order, and indirectly in the case of man."[27] As Lewis Ford stressed, God is more of a cosmic persuader, who lures the actual out of potential by final causality, the way one is drawn by an object of their love.[28]

In one sense the origin or "creation" of the universe is *ex materia* (out of preexisting "stuff"). But the eternal "stuff" is not material but is the realm of eternal forms or potentials that are available for God to order and to urge them to ingress in the ongoing world process as various aspects of actual entities. Since the realm of eternal objects is God's primordial nature, the movement of creation is also *ex Deo*, that is, out of God's potential pole into his actual pole (the world). Reality moves from the unconscious to the conscious, from potential to actual, from abstract to concrete, from forms to facts.

What is it that prompts this movement; what actualizes it? The answer is *creativity*. "Creativity is the principle of *novelty*." Creativity introduces novelty into the actual world. "The 'creative advance' is the application of this ultimate principle of creativity to each novel situation that it originates." Even God is grounded in creativity. For "every actual entity, including God, is a creature transcended by the creativity that it qualifies." Hence, "all actual entities share with God this character of self-causation."[29]

In brief, there is a self-caused movement in God from his potential pole to his actual pole. God is a self-caused "being" who is constantly becoming. Thus the process of creation is an eternal ongoing process of God's self-realization. Hartshorne says clearly: "God in his concrete *de facto* state is in one sense simply self-made, like every creature spontaneously springing into being as something more than any causal antecedents could definitely imply. In another sense, or causally speaking, God, in his latest concrete state, is jointly 'made' or produced by God and the world in the prior states of each. *We are not simply co-creators with God of the world, but in the last analysis co-creators with him of himself.*"[30]

The Nature of Evil

Since God is only relatively perfect, his growth toward perfection is never perfect. Thus, evil is always part of the universe. Or, to put it another way, "There is no reason . . . to conceive the actual world as purely orderly, or as purely chaotic." In fact, "the immanence of God gives reason for belief that pure chaos is intrinsically impossible."[31] God is doing all he can to achieve the most possible out of every moment in world history. "The image under which this operative growth of God's nature is best conceived is that of a tender care that nothing be lost."[32] Evil is what is incompatible with these divine efforts at any given moment. Since God does not force the world, but only persuades it, he cannot destroy evil. He must simply work with it and do the best he can to overcome it.

God's self-realization is never perfect nor is it totally incomplete. In short, divine persuasion responds to the problem of evil radically, simply denying that God exercises full control over the world. Plato sought to express this by saying that God does the best job he can in trying to persuade a recalcitrant matter to receive the impress of the divine forms.[33]

According to Whitehead, "the nature of evil is that the character of things are mutually obstructive."[34] So what a finite God cannot persuade to fit into the overall unity of the actual world is evil. Evil is incompatibility. It is incongruent. Evil is like the leftover pieces of glass that did not fit into the stained-glass window. Only we must remember that the "picture" (order) of the world changes every split second, and what does not fit one moment may fit the next.

The Nature of Human Free Choice

Hartshorne contends that evil or tragedy is rooted in freedom or creativity. Thus, "All free creatures are inevitably more or less dangerous to other creatures, and the most free creatures are the most dangerous."[35] But along with the potential abuse of freedom comes the potential opportunities of freedom. Therefore, "the ideal cannot be to eliminate risk of evil once for all, since this would eliminate novel opportunities for good as well, and would call an arbitrary halt to further realization of the inexhaustible possibilities of good."[36]

With universal freedom comes universal risk. God could guarantee no more or no less.

According to Whitehead, man is a personal being with his own free choice. All people have their own "subjective aims." That is, they purpose ends; they have final causality. God gives overall aim to the world and he provides an initial subjective aim or thrust for all things. That is, "God furnishes the initial direction, but the creature is responsible for its own actualization."[37]

Schubert Ogden notes that even though God is supremely powerful he cannot "wholly . . . determine the decisions of others." However, "by means of his own free decisions" he can "optimize the limits" of the freedom of others. For "if God allowed others either more or less freedom than they actually have, there would be more chances of evil than of good resulting from their decisions rather than the other way around."[38]

The Arguments for the Panentheistic Model of God

Panentheism offers two basic lines of reasoning in defense of its view of God. They are related. First, there are the reasons for rejecting classical theism. Since the two are intertwined, the panentheistic view emerges from its critique of theism. Although Alfred North Whitehead is the fountainhead of panentheism, the arguments against traditional theism were stated best by his most noted student, Charles Hartshorne, and Hartshorne's protégé, Schubert Ogden. Their arguments are put in the form of antinomies (logical contradictions) they see within classical theism. The response to each of these will be given from the classical theist's perspective, Aquinas being the chief representative (see chapter 2).

The Alleged Antinomy of Creation

Schubert Ogden insists that if God is a necessary being and yet his will is one with essence, then creation cannot flow freely from God as classical theists would have it. Hence, if creation is free, then God cannot be a necessary being. For if God necessarily willed creation, as his nature demands, then he was not free in creating.

Classical theism anticipated this objection. Aquinas's answer to this is simple and to the point. "As to things willed by God, we must observe that he wills something of absolute necessity; but this is not true of all that he wills." For example, "God wills the being of his own goodness necessarily. . . . But God wills things other than himself insofar as they are ordered to his own goodness as their ends."[39] That is to say, God is necessary goodness, and this he must will necessarily. All other things are contingent and their goodness is willed contingently. For whatever is in God's nature is there necessarily, but it is not in the nature of God that everything flow from him necessarily. Therefore, God can be a necessary being and yet creation can flow from him freely. Thus, the panentheist's objection fails to show a real contradiction in the classical theist's position on God's nature and creation.

The Alleged Antinomy of Service

According to Ogden there is no meaningful sense in which the traditional God of theism can be served. Service is doing something *for* God. But according to classical theists God is immutably perfect, and thus there is tangibly nothing one can do *for* him. What can we give to a being who literally has everything? For Ogden, the God of theism is "statically completed perfection." So there is nothing we can add to God.

In response, first of all, Ogden misunderstands classical theism at this point. God is not "statically completed perfection." Rather, he is dynamic Act, pure Actuality. Second, Aquinas would admit that one cannot literally add perfection to the nature of the absolutely perfect being God is. But classical theists point out that this does not mean that we cannot do anything "for" God. A perfect God does not *need* our service, but he does *want* it. The Scriptures tell us that "true worshipers will worship the Father in spirit and truth, for the Father seeks such as these to worship Him" (John 4:23, NRSV). What, then, can we give to the God who has everything? Worship. Service. Why? Because he wants it for his glory and for our good. Finally, it is utterly presumptuous for a finite and imperfect creature to think that he can add anything to the infinitely perfect Creator. It is, however, humbling to know that such an exalted being even *wants* (though doesn't *need*) our service to achieve his ends in furthering his kingdom.

The Argument From Existential Repugnance

Another argument given against classical theism is that from "existential repugnance," and it is an outgrowth of the second antinomy. As Ogden states it, "If what we do and suffer as men in the world is from God's perspective wholly indifferent, that perspective is at most irrelevant to our actual existence. It can provide no motive for action, no cause to serve, and no comfort in our distress beyond the motives, causes, and comforts already supplied by our various secular undertakings." But, "More than that, to involve ourselves in these undertakings and to affirm their ultimate significance is to deny the God [of classical theism] who is himself finally conceived as the denial of our life in the world." Hence, classical theism undercuts modern man's belief in "the importance of the secular"—that is, his affirmation "that man and the world are themselves of ultimate significance." Thus one must reject classical theism as existentially repugnant.[40]

In reply, the mistake here is assuming that the God of theism is "wholly indifferent" to our suffering." This does not follow logically from any of the traditional attributes of God. As noted earlier (in chapter 2), the fact that God is impassable (without passion) does not mean he is without feeling. God has unchanging feelings of sympathy for suffering and an immutable feeling of anger at sin. Further, the theistic God became Incarnate in the person of Christ, who experienced our suffering and pain personally. In this sense, God the Son even knows how it feels personally to experience suffering and pain *as a human being*. Of course, *as God* he does not experience changing suffering and pain, since he is impassable (see chapter 2). The two natures in Christ must be distinguished. For, as God, Christ does not change (Malachi 3:6), but as man "he grew in wisdom and stature" (Luke 2:52).

The Alleged Antinomy of Relationship

According to Ogden, the God of traditional theism is unrelatable to the world. For all genuine relationships involve give-and-take, or mutual dependence. According to Aquinas, the world is dependent on God, but God is not dependent on the world. But if God is completely independent of the world, then he is unrelatable with the world. He cannot really interact with the world as the Bible describes him doing.[41]

Here again, theists agree that God is not dependent on the world, but they would deny that this means God cannot have a real relationship with the world. To claim, as Ogden does, that all true relationships involve mutual dependence is wrong. It is a gross anthropomorphism. Just because all real relationships among creatures involve mutual dependence does not mean that this is so of a creature's relation to his Creator. Further, Aquinas showed clearly that there is a *real* relationship between creatures and Creator; it is simply not a relationship in which God depends on his creatures (see chapter 2). The pillar and man are truly related when man is on the right side of it and truly related when man moves to the left side. But it is man who changes, not the pillar. Likewise, God enters into real relationships with changing creatures, but he does not change; they do.

The Alleged Antinomy of Supreme Reality

Charles Hartshorne objects to classical theism on the grounds that either God must include all reality or else he cannot be supreme. He concluded, "The supposition that the supreme reality is not all-inclusive implies that it is but a constituent of the totality, and so not the supreme reality after all."[42]

This objection is based on an equivocal use of the phrase "include all reality." If it means God must include all reality in his *being* (essence), then classical theists would reject it, since creatures are not part of the essence of God. Furthermore, if this is what it means, then Hartshorne has begged the question in favor of his panentheism (God-in-all). If, on the other hand, "include all reality" means include it either in himself or *in his power*, then classical theists would agree. For all reality preexists in its cause (God) either actually (as does God's own essence) or potentially (as does creation). That is, God has the active power (ability) to create something other than himself. In this sense, he is all-inclusive. On the other hand, God is not identical with creation. If he were, he would be both created and uncreated, necessary and contingent, which is impossible. Finally, Hartshorne's objection is based on a univocal concept of being, whereas traditional theists like Aquinas showed that being is to be understood analogically. If being is different in Creator and creatures, then their being is not the same as his. Therefore, Hartshorne's objection fails. For when Aquinas says the world is *in* God, he does not mean it *is* God. It preexists in his power, but it does not coexist with his nature. That is to say, creation is dependent on God, but being finite, it is not identical with God.

The Alleged Antinomy of Contingent Truth

Hartshorne also rejects traditional theism because he believes there is a contradiction in the theistic God who, on the one hand, is held to be without accidental properties and yet, on the other hand, is said to have knowledge of contingent truth. Thus he knows that a certain world exists that might not have existed. But still, none of his properties or qualities are admitted to be contingent![43]

Again, this problem was not unknown to classical theists. Aquinas considered it in the thirteenth century. His response was that all of God's knowledge is necessary, even his knowledge of contingents (see chapter 2). Simply because the *event* is contingent does not mean that God's *knowledge* of it is also contingent. God knows everything that can be known, including the possible and contingent. But he knows them in a necessary way. God can only know in accordance with his own being, and he is a necessary being. Consequently, whatever he knows is known necessarily, even if it is a contingent truth. If God's knowledge were dependent, then his being would be dependent too, since his knowledge is one with his essence. The failure to see this was the error of Molinism.[43]

An Evaluation of Panentheism

Now that we have surveyed the basic panentheistic view of God, some evaluation is in order. Since panentheism offers itself as an alternative to classical theism and is the background for understanding contemporary neotheism, we will concentrate on the areas of overlap in topics.

Some Positive Insights of Panentheism

While panentheism as a total worldview falls short of the mark, it nevertheless offers many insights into the nature of reality.

1. Panentheists are commended for seeking a comprehensive view of reality.

2. Panentheism manages to posit an intimate relation between God and the world without destroying that relation, as pantheism seems to do.

3. Panentheism offers an account of the nature of change.

4. Panentheists acknowledge that there are unchanging elements about reality.

5. Panentheism offers some possible insights into the relationship of the two natures of Christ.

Space and focus do not permit further elaboration here as we have done elsewhere.[44]

A Critique of Panentheism

All its positive insights notwithstanding, as a worldview panentheism fails to make its case. Not only is its critique of classical theism faulty, but it fails to make a positive case for its own view. In fact, rather than attempting to discover who the Christian God really is, it falls into the trap of creating God in its own image.

Panentheists affirm opposite attributes in God. Schubert Ogden, for example, claims that God may be understood as both absolute and relative. Thus God is the "absolutely relative."[45] Also, God is infinitely temporal. Like man, God exists in time, not outside of time. But unlike man, God did not come to exist nor will he ever cease to exist. In this way God is infinitely temporal.[46] Ogden also understands God to be absolutely spatial, or, as Hartshorne would say, all-inclusive. "God's world can comprise nothing less than the sum total of all beings other than himself, both present and past, and his only environment is the wholly internal environment encompassed by his not merely finite but infinite care."[47]

Further, God is both necessary and contingent. He is "the ultimate source and end of all that either is or could ever be." He is "the necessary ground of any and all beings, whether actual or merely possible."[48] Yet God is contingent. He is the all-inclusive and ever changing world order. It is "the world or the universe as a whole" as God's "cosmic body," and his internal relatedness to every nonnecessary creature in the world.[49] But how can God be both of these opposites at the same time?

The panentheist's response is that God has two different natures, so that he is not both in the same sense.[50] But does this really solve the problem? For either God is actually infinite and actually finite at the same time, or he is only one and not the other. But the first option seems contradictory. Indeed, it is contrary to the teaching of panentheism, which affirms that God is only potentially infinite and actually finite. But if God is only actually finite, then the other pole of God is not actual or concrete. In what sense, then, can it be actually part of one God, which panentheism claims to believe? There is nothing actual that holds both poles (natures), the actual and the potential, together. Thus, there is no basis in reality for any unity in God.

Of course, panentheists could affirm that there is one person uniting two different natures, one infinite and the other finite (as in the union of the two natures in the person of Christ). But panentheists have no such uniting center as one "person" with two distinct natures to do this. Indeed, such a concept is contrary to their system, for it would be an enduring "I" that was not subject to the process of change to which they claim all actuality is subject.

One way to solve their dilemma would be to make the two natures of God into two different beings or entities. But in this case they would be dualists, with two different gods. Of course, the door is always open to affirm that beneath all God's diverse activity there is one uniting actuality that does not change. But to affirm this would be to admit the truth of classical theism, namely, that unlimited and unchanging pure Actuality is the ground for everything else that exists, including all the change and diversity in the world.[51]

Panentheism violates the law of causality. According to panentheists, God is actually finite, contingent, dependent, etc. But the fundamental principle of causality demands that every actual contingent being has an actual non-contingent (i.e., a necessary) cause. For if God is actually dependent, then there must be some actually independent being on which he depends. Otherwise, we are sent on a futile infinite regress where every being in the series is dependent, but there is nothing on which they are dependent.

Nor will it suffice to say that God is potentially necessary. A *potentially* necessary being is not an *actual* cause of anything. As a result, panentheism violates the fundamental principle that every finite, dependent being needs a cause beyond it. This leads to another problem.

A self-created being is impossible. Panentheism speaks of God as self-created (see p. 55). By this they mean that God has infinite potential, which he is continually self-actualizing into his actual finite being. But this too appears to be incoherent. For how can a being actualize itself? For God to do so would be to lift himself up by his own bootstraps. Only actuality can actualize. No potentiality can actualize itself any more than cups can fill themselves or than the mere capacity for a suntan can produce a tan. To actualize, one needs to be actual, and to be actualized, one needs to have potential. But one and the same thing cannot be both actual and potential. Hence, it is impossible to self-actualize. For one cannot be both in a state of actuality and potentiality with regard to the same thing. Ultimately, a self-creating or self-actualizing God is impossible.

Panentheists may reply that God is not the cause of his own *being* but simply of his *becoming.* Hence, there is no contradiction. But even in this case there is nothing to actually ground God's becoming, that is, his moment by moment changing from non-being to being (from annihilation to re-creation), which is entailed in the panentheistic view of change. Whitehead posited "creativity" to solve this problem and to provide a grounding for the ever-changing God. But "creativity" is not a being but only an accident of God as an actual entity in his system. Thus it has no ontological status (being) by which it can ground any other being. Of course, one could always endow "creativity" with being and make it the ground of all other being.

But in this case we have reverted to traditional theism's concept of pure Being of Actuality, which is the creative ground of all other beings.

Relative perfection implies absolute perfection. God cannot be merely relatively or progressively perfect. For how could we know God is getting more perfect unless there were a standard of absolute perfection by which he was being measured? In short, we cannot know something is getting better unless we know what is best.[52] But this standard of perfection would either have to be outside of God or inside him (i.e., be God). If the latter, then process theology is falsified. And if the former, then we have reverted to platonism where there is some reality outside God (the Good) that is more ultimate than God. But this is contrary to panentheism, to say nothing of other objections that can be leveled against it. For one, if it *is* the ultimate reality, then why not consider it God? And, in any event, if it is ultimate reality, then all other beings would be real only by somehow participating in it. But this too moves in the direction of classical theism and away from panentheism, which admits no such absolutely perfect being.

Panentheism holds an incoherent view of change. Panentheism asserts that all actuality is changing; all being is in flux. In fact, all "being" is really becoming. But this entails an incoherent view of change. In fact, it turns out to be affirming that there is change but nothing that is changing. It is like saying that it is raining but there are no drops of rain falling. There is motion but nothing moving. It is difficult to make sense of this. In more technical terms, the process view of change reduces to a continual annihilation, re-creation, annihilation, re-creation, etc., every split second. Hartshorne claimed that in "human experiences" these nows "normally" occur some 10–20 per second. At the low rate of ten per second, this would mean there were 200 different "I"s that typed this sentence! And each "I" was annihilated and succeeded by another "I" (I, I, I, I, I, I, etc.). There is no enduring "I" beneath the change. In truth, I did not write this book. If panentheism is correct, there were millions of different "I"s who wrote it! Besides being patently absurd, such a claim is self-defeating. For the very statement that "*I* am really a succession of 'I's" implies by the use of the first "I" in the sentence that there is an enduring "I" throughout the very sentence that affirms that there is no such enduring "I." In short, I would have to be more than a series of "I"s or else I could not even make a meaningful statement such as "I am really a series of 'I's."[53] "So serious is the absence of personal identity and continuity that Hartshorne actually affirms that 'I' ceases to exist in periods of unconscious sleep, and only 'pops' back into selfhood (although as another 'self')."[54] This would mean that people who come out of a coma are actually being reincarnated. Indeed, it would mean that a parent awakening a child from sleep is actually calling him or her back into existence![55]

This View Eliminates Moral Responsibility

As Royce Gruenler noted, "Not only does this take us to the edge of absurdity and render the question of free will moot, but also it brings into question the biblical doctrine that a person is responsible for his or her actions, a doctrine that clearly assumes that one who speaks or acts in a certain way is responsible for that behavior *as the same person.*"[56]

Thus, "Since process theism has no explanation of the enduring self, and indeed denies the identical selfhood of the person from moment to moment, it is academic whether 'I' have freedom of choice as 'I' move into the future of possibility, since my present 'I' will momentarily perish and be superseded by another 'I' that has no substantial continuity with all 'my' previous 'I's."[57] In this way, process theology makes not only a continuous self impossible but a responsible self impossible as well. In effect, it destroys moral responsibility, for it was not "I" but a previous "I" (or series of "I"s) who was or were responsible for the morally responsible act.

Total relativity is not possible. It is difficult to understand how we can know that everything is relative and changing. How could anyone be sure that something is changing without having some unchanging measure to measure the change? And if everything is changing, then there could not be the standard or measure by which we could measure the change. Almost everyone has had the experience of waiting at a traffic signal and wondering whether his car is moving or the one next to it is. If one can see a fixed object, like a building, he can know who is moving. But what if the building is moving? Then we cannot be sure whether we are moving or not. In short, how can a panentheist know that all is relative and changing unless there is something that is not relative and changing? A panentheist might answer that his unchanging measure is the immutable primordial nature of God. But this answer does not seem adequate. For God's primordial pole is only an abstraction or idea that has no extramental reality. So, as such, it cannot be an actual measure, only a conceptual one. Even the flux philosopher Heraclitus posited an unchanging Logos beneath the changing world by which it could be measured.

God as spatial involves great difficulties. The panentheist's belief that God is coextensive with space is fundamentally problematic. For according to modern physics (which panentheism accepts) nothing travels faster than the speed of light in space. If so, then God could not apprehend the whole universe at once. For his mind could not travel across the universe any faster than 186,000+ miles per second. But by the time he has moved from one end of the universe to the other, the universe would have changed multimillions upon trillions of times. In this case God would not really know the universe (his "body") at all. He could only know an infinitesimal portion at a time while all else is changing. As one former process theologian put it, "The incontestable fact is that if God moves necessarily in time he is limited to some rate of velocity that is finite (say, the speed of light, if not the faster rate of some hypothetical tachyon)." And, "This means, unfortunately for process theism, that it is impossible for such a finite deity to have a simultaneous God's-eye view of the whole universe at once, since it would take him millions of light years or more to receive requisite data from distant points and places."[58]

Of course, panentheists could solve their problem by affirming that God's mind transcends the universe and is not subject to the speed of light. But if they take this way out of the dilemma, they fall right into the arms of classical theism, which they strongly reject. So the painful alternative for panentheism is to retain an incoherent view or else return to theism.

God as limited in knowledge is seriously problematic. Since the panentheist holds that God is limited in his knowledge, he does not know the future with certainty. Indeed, he cannot know what we will do with our free choice. This being the case, he can have no fixed overall plan toward which everything flows with assurance. Indeed, panentheists once frankly admitted that God himself is "waiting with bated breath" to see how things will turn out. But if God does not even know the future, to say nothing of controlling it, then he cannot guarantee its outcome.

Panentheism guarantees no resolution of the problem of evil. Since God is finite and struggling, we cannot be assured of any ultimate victory over evil. The best we can hope for is an ongoing eternal struggle. For if evil is only a "misfit" of some actual entity in the ongoing order of the universe, it is always possible that something will not fit. Indeed, what fits at one point may not fit at another. In this sense, there is a kind of regress in some things, even if the overall order is allegedly improving.

But if we have no assurance that good will eventually triumph over evil, then why fight evil? Maybe standing for good will put us on the losing side. Such a belief has a negative motivational value. It does not stir men to the core to join in a battle worth sacrificing all for, since, according to panentheism, we do not know it will eventually be worthwhile and/or victorious.

The panentheistic God lacks true religious worth. The God of process theology is not ultimately good and, hence, does not call for an ultimate commitment. As Paul Tillich pointed out, only what is really ultimate is worthy of an ultimate commitment.[59] To give an ultimate commitment (which is what religion is) to anything less than the Ultimate is idolatry. Panentheists, in fact, worship a finite god. And every finite thing is a creature. For every finite (changing, contingent) thing needs a cause. Only the Creator of all finite things is infinite. And only this infinite Creator is worthy of worship. To worship anything or anyone less than him, that is, something or someone finite, is idolatry. The panentheistic God lacks true worshipability. Or to put it another way, he is not worthy of worship or of an ultimate commitment. As Paul Tillich would say, he is religiously unworthy of our ultimate concern.

Panentheism creates God in its own image. Perhaps the root flaw of process theology is that while God created man in his own image, process theology has returned the compliment. Creating God in the image of man is fraught with all kinds of dangers, metaphysical and moral. Simply because human beings are bipolar, changing, dependent, etc., does not mean that God is. Even process theologians must admit that God is not like us in many ways. Whitehead, for example, said that *only God* is eternal, necessary, nontemporal, and transcends the world (in his primordial nature). In brief, even the panentheistic God is uncreated, eternal, and encompasses all reality. Consequently, there are many significant characteristics possessed by God that humans do not have. Why then should we make God finite, changing, relative, and divisible simply because we are?

The panentheistic view of truth is self-defeating. Panentheism denies absolute truth, insisting that all truth is relative.[60] But the very statement that "all truth is relative" is either an absolute truth or a relative one. If it is absolute, then it is self-defeating, since it makes an absolute truth claim in the very process of affirming that there are no such truths. On the other hand, if it is just another relative truth claim, then there is no reason that we should accept it over any other claim. But, in fact, it makes a tacit claim to be *the* truth about reality, which is an absolute truth. Or, to put it another way, panentheism claims to be true at all times, in all places, and for all people. But this by definition is an absolute truth, as opposed to a relative truth, which is only true at some times, places, and/or for some people. Therefore, panentheism makes an absolute truth claim that all truth is relative, which is self-defeating.

Of course, a panentheist could claim that all truth claims except theirs are relative. But this begs the question: why can't theists or even atheists make the same claim? Why should special status be given to their relativism as the absolute truth? In fact, as total relativists they stand on the pinnacle of their own presumed absolute to relativize everything else. And in the process of so doing they destroy their own claim to relativism by their presumed absolutism.

A Final Word

Both classical theists and neotheists reject panentheism as a total system. However, neotheists (the subject of the remaining chapters) do not reject it entirely. In fact, neotheists agree with panentheism in significant ways. These will become apparent in the next chapter. It is precisely over this that there is conflict between classical theism and neotheism. This conflict is the subject of the rest of this book. It has both doctrinal and important practical consequences for the Christian church.

CHAPTER FOUR

THE
BIBLICAL CLAIMS
OF
NEOTHEISM

The question of the nature of God is the most fundamental in all of theology. On it stands or falls all other major doctrines. From its very inception, orthodox Christianity has been uncompromisingly theistic. Recently, this venerable history has been seriously challenged by an admittedly new view, which claims to be Christian but zealously desires to make major changes in the classical theistic view. Several proponents of this view (Clark Pinnock, Richard Rice, John Sanders, William Hasker, and David Basinger) have collaborated on a volume titled *The Openness of God* (InterVarsity Press, 1994). All of these scholars had previously written works of their own on the topic.[1] Other Christian thinkers share similar views or have expressed sympathy for this position.[2]

Proponents have variously labeled their view "The Openness of God View" or "Free Will Theism." Others have called this new theism a form of process theology or panentheism because of its important similarities to this position (see chapter 3). But it seems more appropriate to call it neotheism for several reasons. First, it has significant differences from the panentheism of Whitehead, Hartshorne, and company. Neotheism, like classical theism, affirms many of the essential attributes of God, including infinity, necessity, ontological independence, transcendence, omniscience, omnipotence, and omnipresence. Likewise, it shares with traditional theism the belief in *ex nihilo* creation and direct divine supernatural intervention in the world. Since process theology denies all these, it seems unfair to list neotheism as a subspecies of that view.

On the other hand, since there are significant differences between the new theism and classical theism, neither does it fit comfortably in the theistic category. For example, neotheism denies God's immutability, eternality, simplicity, and pure actuality.

In addition, it denies God's foreknowledge of future free acts, and as a consequence, God's complete sovereignty over human events. These are serious enough deviations from a bimillennial Christian view to deserve another name, as well as to arouse interest in the topic.

Perhaps one should simply accept the self-label "Openness of God View" or "Free Will Theism." However, this is neither necessary nor desirable for several reasons. For one thing, neither title is really descriptive or simple. Classical theism also affirms free will. And the title "Openness of God View" is cumbersome and not distinctly descriptive. Open to what? Open in what way? It seems better to call the view what it is and claims to be, namely, a significant modification of traditional theism in the direction of process theology or panentheism. Thus, we have called it new theism or neotheism. Indeed, it offers itself as a third alternative to both theism and panentheism.[3] Call it what one may, this view is a serious challenge to classical theism, and with it, a serious threat to many important doctrines and practices built on that view (see chapter 7).

As the new kid on the block, neotheism desires to make itself clear, distinct, and appealing. Since neotheists desire to be members of the broad theistic camp, they have understandably put their best foot forward in describing their view. Let's examine the distinctives of their proposal.

The Distinctives of Neotheism

Neotheists list five characteristics of their position: "1. God not only created this world *ex nihilo* but can and at times does intervene unilaterally in earthly affairs. 2. God chose to create us with incompatibilistic (libertarian)[4] freedom—freedom over which he cannot exercise total control. 3. God so values freedom—the moral integrity of free creatures and a world in which such integrity is possible—that he does not normally override such freedom, even if he sees that it is producing undesirable results. 4. God always desires our highest good, both individually and corporately, and thus is affected by what happens in our lives. 5. God does not possess exhaustive knowledge of exactly how we will utilize our freedom, although he may very well at times be able to predict with great accuracy the choices we will freely make" (Pinnock, *The Openness of God*, hereafter OG, p. 156).

In order to bring this view into focus, a comparison between theism (chapter 2), panentheism (chapter 3), and neotheism will be helpful. A chart depicting this comparison follows on pages 76–77.

The Alleged Biblical Basis of Neotheism

The proponents of this view offer several lines of evidence in support of their position. But the biblical arguments are fundamental. These are especially crucial to their attempt to show that the Bible supports their view that God is not pure existence (aseity), eternal, immutable, impassable, simple, and capable of foreseeing free acts—all of which characterize the classical theistic view of God.

God's Aseity

Most of the efforts of neotheists to undermine the biblical basis for aseity are focused on Exodus 3:14, namely, God's self-description as "I AM WHO I AM." They agree with the comment of neoorthodox writer Emil Brunner that this is a "disastrous misunderstanding" (OG, 181). Their arguments fall into several categories:

Alleged influence of Hellenic thought. The traditional interpretation of this text is said to be wrong because "it came from Hellenic thought with its quest to find that which escapes the ravages of time" (OG, 99). Besides being a genetic fallacy, and psychoanalysis rather than exegesis, this allegation as such offers no real argument in favor of an alternative interpretation. Nonetheless, it will be discussed in more detail later (in the next section). Here the concern is whether the biblical text teaches the attributes of a theistic God.

Alleged neglect of other texts. Neotheists draw attention to the fact that "biblical statements such as 'I AM WHO I AM' (Exodus 3:14) are understood [by classical theists] to express the true divine nature as atemporal and pure actuality, while statements that describe God as the 'one who is, and who was, and who is to come' (Revelation 1:4)

	THEISM	NEOTHEISM	PANENTHEISM
GOD'S ATTRIBUTES	Nontemporal	Temporal	Temporal
	Simple	Complex	Complex
	Pure actuality	Actuality and potentiality	Actuality and potentiality
	Unchangeable will	Changeable will	Changeable will
	Unqualified omniscience	Qualified omniscience	Not omniscient
	Foreknowledge of freedom	No certain foreknowledge of free acts	No foreknowledge of free acts
	Cannot learn anything	Can learn something	Can learn many things
	Unchangeable nature	Changeable nature	Changeable nature
	Infinite	Infinite & Eternal	Finite
	Omnipotent	Omnipotent	Not omnipotent
GOD/WORLD RELATIONSHIP	Independent of the world	Independent of the world	Mutual dependence on the world
NATURE OF CREATION	Ex nihilo (out of nothing)	Ex nihilo (out of nothing)	Ex materia (out of something)
RISK OF CREATION	None	Some	Much

	THEISM	NEOTHEISM	PANENTHEISM
GOD'S SOVEREIGNTY	Complete control	Overall control	No control
DIVINE ACTION ON FREE ACTS	Highly persuasive (or coercive)	Moderately persuasive (never coercive)	Lightly persuasive (never coercive)
DIVINE INTERVENTION IN CREATION	Occasional miracles	Occasional miracles	No miracles
PROVIDENCE	Specific	General (from without)	General (from within)
PETITIONARY PRAYER	Does not change God's will or nature	Does change God's will, not his essential nature	Does change God's will and nature
FUTURE	Completely determined	Determined in general	Completely undetermined
EVIL	Planned and could have been prevented	Only permitted and could have been prevented	Not planned and could not have been prevented
DETERMINISM/FREE WILL	Compatible	Incompatible	Incompatible
FOREKNOWLEDGE OF FREE ACTS	What will and could happen	What will, not could, happen	Neither what will nor what could happen
GOD'S KNOWLEDGE	Complete: past, present, and future	Complete: past & present; partial of future	Partial: past, present, and future

are ignored or written off as figures of speech" (OG, 99).

In response, it should be noted first of all that one cannot avoid the teaching of one text by diverting the issue to what is said in another text. While all Scripture is consistent, the meaning of one text cannot be dictated by what is said in another context.

What is more, the Revelation 1:4 text does not contradict Exodus 3:14. For to claim that God always "is" does not imply that he does not exist in the past, present, and future. On the contrary, it declares that he *always is*. It simply affirms that God cannot grow old; he has no age. He forever *is*. Or, to borrow some phrases from one of the neotheists: "Though we wither and die, God abides and is not threatened or undone by time." That is, "God transcends our experience of time, is immune from the ravages of time . . ." (OG, 120). But this is at the heart of what theists affirm about God's nontemporality. Likewise, if God transcends all beings that have the potentiality to change, then he must have no potentiality to change. That is, he must be a being of pure actuality and aseity as well.

Furthermore, suppose there was a conflict between the two passages. Assuming there is not a contradiction in Scripture, the question is which passages must be taken literally (metaphysically) and which should not. Two hermeneutical clues indicate that God really is the "I AM," viz., the eternal, self-existent One.

First of all, in the Exodus passage it was specifically asked, "What is his name [character, essence]?" (Exodus 3:13). Whereas, Revelation 1:4 is simply John's description of the God who from a temporal vantage point always was, is, and is to come.

When God speaks through John in the Revelation 1:4 passage, he is described as "him who *is*" (present tense) and "who *was*" (past tense) and "who is to come" (future tense). Indeed, he *is* in the past; he *is* in the present, and he *is* in the future. As a matter of fact, he always *is*.

Finally, when two passages appear to conflict, the one to be taken literally is the one that can best explain the other not being taken literally. For example, John 4:24 says, "God is spirit." Yet God is described as having eyes, arms, legs, and as being a tower, a rock, and even a bird with wings (passim). Now it is clear, even to the neotheist, that God is literally a spirit and these other words must be understood figuratively. It makes no sense to say he is literally all these other things and figuratively a spirit. It is not an unusual practice to understand some things in the Bible figuratively. Even neotheists admit that when there are conflicting texts, one must be taken literally and the other figuratively (OG, 17). What they have not done is provide a convincing case for why Exodus 3:14—a text claiming to give the very essence of who God is—should not be taken as a literal declaration of his self-existence.

Appeal to modern linguists. Neotheists appeal to current trends among linguists to interpret Exodus 3:14 as "I will be who I will be." But this linguistic possibility must be rejected for many reasons. For one, the context opposes it, since God is asked to give his "name" (character or essence).

Two, the history of both Jewish and Christian interpretation of this text is overwhelmingly in favor of the classical interpretation. Neotheists reluctantly acknowledge this, combing through church history to find teachers here and there on this or that who may agree with them. The truth is that nearly all the great patristic, medieval, and reformation theologians understood Exodus 3:14 as an affirmation of God's self-existence (aseity).

Three, the Greek translation of the Old Testament, the Septuagint (LXX), as even neotheism proponents admit, favors the traditional aseity view. It translates the Hebrew "I AM WHO I AM" (*ekyeh ser ehyeh*) as "he who is" (*ho on*).

Four, the rendering "I will be who I will be," while grammatically possible, is contextually implausible and historically late, emerging in the wake of process theology. Ironically, for those who claim classical theism was influenced by the (Greek) philosophy of its day, it turns out that their view arose in a climate dominated by the (process) philosophy of our day.

Five, the very name Yahweh (YHWH), usually translated LORD in the Old Testament is probably a contraction of "I AM WHO I AM." Old Testament commentator R. Alan Cole says, "This pithy clause is clearly a reference to the name YHWH. Probably 'Yahweh' is regarded as a shortening of the whole phrase, and a running together of the clause into one word."[5] Even *The Theological Dictionary of the Old Testament* acknowledges that "the name is generally thought to be a verbal form derived from the root *hwy*, later *hyh*, 'be at hand, *exist*, come to pass.''[6] Arthur Preuss summed it up well: "The more general and more ancient opinion among theologians favors the view that aseity constitutes the metaphysical essence of God. Hence, we shall act prudently in adopting this theory, especially since it is well founded in Holy Scripture and tradition, and can be defended with solid philosophical arguments.... Sacred Scripture defines YHWH as *ho on*, and it would seem, therefore, that this definition is entitled to universal acceptance.''[7]

Six, this process and neotheistic understanding is contrary to Jesus' use of it in John 8:58: "Before Abraham was born, I am!" Notice Jesus did not affirm: "Before Abraham was, I will be who I will be," as he should have if the process understanding of this text is correct. For a follower of Christ, Jesus' understanding of this text should be definitive.

Finally, even if it could be proven that Exodus 3:14 does not support the claim of God for self-existence, there are plenty of other texts and good arguments that do. The very concept of God as uncreated Creator (Genesis 1:1) who brought all other things into existence (John 1:1–3; Colossians 1:15–16; Hebrews 1:2) is sufficient to prove his self-existence. And even neotheists claim to believe in *ex nihilo* creation, affirming that "the triune God is the Creator of the world out of nothing" (OG, 109). And reason demands that if God is Creator of all things, then he was uncreated. And if he did not obtain his existence from another, then he must exist in and of himself (aseity).

In brief, there is strong evidence that Exodus 3:14 supports God's aseity. But even if it does not, there is ample support elsewhere for this venerable theistic position. Thus, there are no real grounds, biblical or otherwise, for the denial of this long-held attribute of God.

Eternality (Nontemporality)

Neotheism also rejects the concept of a nontemporal God, which has been part of theism from the earliest times. The biblical reasons given by neotheists for rejecting God's eternality have to do with the fact that God is continually referred to in Scripture as acting in time.

God's acts of creation were in time (Genesis 1–2), as were his acts of redemption (cf. Exodus 12:1f and John 1:10–14). If God was in time at the Exodus, then there was a time before that and a time after that. And whatever being has a before and after is a temporal being. Also, the Bible sometimes refers to God as having a past, present, and future. He is the one "who is, and who was, and who is to come" (Revelation 1:8). Indeed, the very words for God being eternal (*ainonos, ainonios*) can mean age or ages. So, God is "eternal" in the sense of being in endless time.

Several comments are in order in response. First, these objections to God's timelessness are based on a confusion of his *actions* with his *attributes*. God is beyond time, but his actions are in time. This should not be difficult for neotheists to understand, since they believe God is infinite and yet acts in the finite world. God is Creator and yet acts in creation without being a creature. Why, then, cannot God act in time without being temporal?

Second, this objection overlooks the fact that the Bible clearly affirms that God is the Creator of time who, by that very fact, is himself beyond time. Hebrews 1:2 speaks of God "framing the ages" or time. But if he is Creator of time, then he cannot be in time. Jude 25 says Christ was "before all ages." But clearly he who was before the temporal world is not himself temporal. In John, Jesus spoke of the glory he had with the Father "before the world began" (John 17:5). The Bible also uses parallel phrases, such as "before the foundation of the world" (Ephesians 1:4, NKJV). Paul spoke emphatically of grace "given us in Christ Jesus *before the beginning of time*" (2 Timothy 1:9). But if time began, then God is not part of it, since he has no beginning or end.

Simplicity

Another attribute of God under attack by the new theism is that of simplicity. Classical theists appeal to the fact that God is incorruptible (Romans 1:23, NKJV) and immortal (1 Timothy 6:16) to show that he is a simple, indivisible being. For only what has parts can be torn apart or corrupted. Likewise, God is spirit (John 4:24) and not matter (Luke 24:39), which can be divided. Indeed, God's pure actuality (Exodus 3:14) reveals that he is a simple being, since he has no potentiality to change.

Neotheists reject the attribute of simplicity, basing their argument largely on the verses that indicate that God changes. Since immutability is the next attribute to be discussed, only brief comments will be made here on viewing God as a complex being. *First, it is contrary to the Scriptures, which reveal that God is not divisible.* Second, if God were divisible, he would not be absolutely one, as the Bible indicates that he is (Deuteronomy 6:4; 1 Corinthians 8:4). Third, serious philosophical problems result from denying God's simplicity. For example, if God is a complex being, then he has "parts." What holds these parts together? And is he then simple? If God has parts, why can he not come apart (i.e., be destroyed)? Is it not possible for what is composed to also decompose? If not, then what holds the parts together? And would not this have to be both simple and uncomposed? In short, to affirm complexity in God seems to be based on the assumption that there is a deeper unity that holds the complexity together. But this deeper indivisible unity is precisely what classical theists claim, namely, that God in his very essence is simple and indivisible.

Immutability

Another crucial attribute in dispute is God's immutability. The neotheists insist that God can change. Again, the whipping boy is Greek philosophy and the villain is an alleged misinterpretation of Exodus 3:14. Neotheists affirm that "this text, which points to the living God of the Exodus, was transmuted into a principle of metaphysical immutability, as the dynamic 'I AM' of the Hebrew text became the impersonal 'being who is there' of the Greek Septuagint (LXX)" (OG, 106). Several biblical arguments are offered in favor of a mutable God.

God is presented as changing. Well known to disputants on both sides of the issue are several Scripture passages describing God as repenting or changing his mind (cf. Genesis 6:6; 1 Samuel 15:11). Defenders of God's immutability take these as "anthropomorphisms," expressions that depict God in a human way for our un-

derstanding. Stephen Charnock in his classic work on God's attributes is typical: "God is not changed when loving any creatures he
becomes angry with them, or when angry he becomes appeased. The
change in these cases is in the creature; according to the alteration
in the creature, it stands in various relations to God" (OG, 28).
Neotheists reject these explanations, insisting that these expressions
should be taken literally, not figuratively. They point to the fact that
any references that speak of God as unchanging are rare compared
to the many times God is represented as changing.

This, however, is a less than convincing objection. For one thing,
they themselves admit that there are anthropomorphisms in the
Bible that depict God with arms, legs, eyes, and even wings—none
of which they take literally. How do they know? This they rightly do
because other less abundant verses of Scripture assert that God is a
spirit (John 4:24) which does not have a physical body (Luke 24:39).
But if these cannot be taken literally because they conflict with other
clear statements, then why should this not also be the assertion when
God is depicted as changing his mind? This leads to a second point.

Even neotheists acknowledge that there are some texts that speak
of God as not changing or repenting. For example, Moses wrote:
"God is not a man, that he should lie, nor a son of man that he
should repent" (Numbers 23:19, KJV). Malachi 3:6 declares: "I the
LORD do not change." The writer of Hebrews declared that "it is
impossible for God to lie" (Hebrews 6:18). Paul also spoke of the
"God who cannot lie" (Titus 1:2, KJV) and assured us that "if we are
faithless, he remains faithful; he cannot deny Himself" (2 Timothy
2:13, NKJV). And 1 Samuel 15:29 affirms emphatically, "He who is
the Glory of Israel does not lie or change his mind; for he is not a
man, that he should change his mind." What is more, this is affirmed
in the very context that states that God does change his mind, something that the author of 1 Samuel thought to be consistent (15:11).
But this could only be the case if one of these two is taken literally
and the other not. But which is which? Once again the answer comes
only by seeing which is best explained in the light of the other. This
is just an example of the venerable principle of the analogy of Scripture, that Scripture interprets Scripture. And it is easier to understand God as apparently changing in the light of his actually un-

changing nature, rather than the reverse. For his "regret" (15:11, NKJV) for having set up Saul as king is obviously connected to a change in Saul's behavior, not a change in God. And the affirmation that he does not change is made in connection with who he is and, thus, why he can be trusted.

The Charge of Falsehood on God

Many times in the Bible God says he will do one thing but then does another. For example, he said through Jonah (3:4) that he would overturn Nineveh in forty days, but he did not (3:10). Neotheists claim that this implies that God must have changed. Otherwise, we must assume that God lied. Proponents write: "God will not say one thing while fully intending to do something else." For, "Unlike human beings, God will not say one thing and then arbitrarily do another" (OG, 33).

Actually, neotheists unwittingly answer their own objection for a couple of reasons. First of all, the assertion that God is not "arbitrary" implies that he is unchanging in his will. But this is the very thing they are denying.

Second, the fact that they are sure that "God *never* says one thing while fully intending to do something else" (emphasis added) also reveals a belief that he does not change. Otherwise, how could they know that is true?

Third, their objection overlooks the conditional nature of Jonah's message. It is clear that Jonah's exhortation to Nineveh implied *if you do not repent, you will perish*. Otherwise, the offer for repentance would not have been genuine and God could be charged with deception—the very thing neotheists wish to avoid doing. Also, the fact that Nineveh did repent and Jonah was displeased (4:1) reveals that he believed the message was conditional. For after they repented and God spared them, "Jonah was greatly displeased and became angry. He prayed to the LORD. . . . That is why I was so quick to flee to Tarshish. I knew that you are a gracious and compassionate God, slow to anger and abounding in love, a God who relents from sending calamity (Jonah 4:1–2).

Finally, in every case in Scripture where God announces one

thing and then does another it is either in the context of desiring a change in someone's activity or else using them to bring about change. This is true whether it is the repentance of Nineveh or the mediation of Moses to which we now turn.

Petitionary Prayer Implies an Actual Change in God

Proponents of neotheism argue that petitionary prayer entails a real change in God. Appeal is often made to Abraham's barter with God (Genesis 18:16–33) or with Moses' intercession to save Israel (Exodus 32:7–14). In the latter case, they reason that "the fact is that God relents in direct response to Moses' plea, not as a consequence of the people's repentance of their apostasy." Thus, "The repentance mentioned in this case clearly applies to a change that took place in God, not in his people" (OG, 28). Further, they argue that "the assurance that God will *not* repent presupposes the general possibility that God *can* repent when he chooses" (OG, 33).

This objection, however, falls short of its mark for a number of reasons. First of all, it is contorted logic to affirm that God's unchangeableness implies that he could change. Does this mean that God's faithfulness to his nature and to his Word imply that he could be unfaithful to it? Does this mean when the Scripture affirms that "God cannot lie" (Titus 1:2 cf. Hebrews 6:18) that it implies he can lie? What about when the Word of God declares that "if we are faithless, he will remain faithful, for he cannot disown himself (2 Timothy 2:13)? Does this mean God could be unfaithful?

Second, even neotheism admits that "God's essential nature and his ultimate purpose did not change—Moses' appeal presupposes this" (OG, 28). But if God's "essential nature" did not change (which is precisely what classical theists contend), then God did not change in his essence. For "essential nature" is precisely what classical theists mean by "essence." Nonessential nature, whatever that may mean, is not part of the essence of God.[8]

Further, neotheists even acknowledge that God's "ultimate objectives" did not change. So, neither God's nature nor purpose changed. Why, then, speak of a change *in God*? Ironically, they hint at the answer themselves when they add, "His [God's] ultimate objectives require him to change his immediate intentions" (OG, 28). Had they used the word "tactics" instead of "intentions," no classical theist would object. With unchanging nature and unvarying ultimate intention, God uses various means to accomplish his immutable will. In this case, it was Moses' prayer that God ordained as the means by which he would accomplish his ultimate will to deliver his people. There is no need to say God's essence changed in order to fully explain this or any other passage of Scripture.

The neotheistic objection also fails to take into account that simply because the people of Israel did not repent does not mean there was no change at all that occasioned God's apparent change of plan for Israel. There was a change in Moses. As leader and mediator for his people, there was a change in Moses' heart, which allowed God's unchanging mercy to flow to Israel through Moses as their mediator. For God has ordained that his mercy is released through calling on him to help. Like any good parent, he wants to be asked. Suppose, for example, that a concerned mother knows in advance that her fevered child will awake later in the night crying for help. In anticipation, she places water and aspirin by her bedside. But she does not administer the help until the child awakes and cries for it. Even so, our heavenly Father who knows "the end from the beginning" (Isaiah 46:10) often waits for us to call on him before he responds, whether it is for ourselves or for someone else.

Finally, even in the case of Moses' intercession there is evidence of God's unchanging will. For Moses reminded God of his promise to Israel, saying, "Remember your servants Abraham, Isaac and Israel, to whom you swore by your own self: 'I will make your descendants as numerous as the stars in the sky and I will give your descendants all this land I promised them, and it will be their inheritance forever' " (Exodus 32:13). No conditions were attached to this promise. Indeed, Abraham was not even conscious when God's promise was unilaterally ratified by God (Genesis 15). So, Moses was simply praying the promise of God, reminding God of what he had promised to do. Effective prayer is, as John said, asking in God's will (John 15:7). Prayer is not a means by which we get our will done in heaven. Rather, it is a means by which God gets his will done on earth. It is utterly presumptuous for mortal man to believe that their prayer actually changes God. Instead, prayer is a means by which God changes us and others.

The Allegation That God Sometimes Rejects What He Has Done

Proponents of the new theism assert that "God repents in a variety of circumstances. Sometimes God rejects something that he has already done. 'And the LORD was sorry that he had made humankind on the earth, and it grieved him to his heart' (Genesis 6:6, NRSV)" (OG, 27). This, they insist, implies a change in God.

However, this allegation overlooks several important things. For one thing, Genesis 6:6 does not use the same Hebrew word for "repent" as does 1 Samuel 15:29. Samuel uses *shaqar*, which means that God will not cheat, lie, deceive, break a covenant, act falsely, or be untrue. But the Hebrew word *nacham* used in Genesis 6:6 is translated "sorry" (NRSV). It means to be "grieved" (NIV), to sigh, breathe strongly, groan, be sorry. It reflects God's feeling toward mankind's sin, not a change in his thinking.

What is more, since the contrast in this text is with a state of innocence in which God created mankind (cf. Genesis 1:27; 3:5, 22) and their perverted state just before the flood (Genesis 6:5), it is speaking about God's feelings toward *different things*. Or, better yet, it is not speaking about different feelings God has about the same thing, but different feelings he has toward different things. God always has the same consistent feeling toward the same thing. As an unchangingly holy God, he always feels grieved about sin and unvaryingly good about his perfect creation (Genesis 1:31). So the change is not in God but in man. Thus, another crucial proof text for neotheism fails to accomplish its purpose.

Omniscience. The new theism also rejects the classical concept of omniscience in favor of a limited form of foreknowledge. While the formal definition is the same, the actual knowledge is different. That is, God is said to be omniscient in principle but not in practice. He can know everything that is knowable, but he cannot know what future free acts will bring about. Several biblical arguments are offered in support of this conclusion.

The Allegation That God Learns

Neotheists contend that the Bible sometimes describes God as learning through experience. For instance, God said to Abraham after he proved his willingness to offer Isaac: "Now I know that you fear God, because you have not withheld from me your son, your only son" (Genesis 22:12). According to neotheism, this verse implies that God did not know how Abraham would respond to his command, since it was only after Abraham obeyed that God said, "Now I know that you fear God."

However, the problem with this interpretation is twofold. First, this understanding is not necessary in the context. Second, it is contrary to what the rest of Scripture reveals about God. The passage begins by stating that "God tested Abraham" (v. 1). There is nothing here about God's desire to *learn* anything. Rather, God wanted to *prove* something (cf. 2 Chronicles 32:31). What God knew by *cognition*, he desired to show by *demonstration*. By passing the test, Abraham demonstrated what God always knew: namely, that he feared God. For example, a math teacher might say to her class, "Let's see if we can find the square root of 49," and then, after demonstrating it, declare, "Now we know that the square root of 49 is 7," even though she knew from the beginning what the answer was. Even so, God, who knows all things cognitively from the beginning, could appropriately say after Abraham had proved his faith, "Now I know [demonstratively] that you fear God."

Furthermore, since the Bible does not contradict itself, what might otherwise be a possible interpretation of this text is eliminated by the clear teaching of Scripture elsewhere. Namely, God is infinite in understanding (Psalm 147:5, NKJV); he knows "the end from the beginning" (Isaiah 46:10) and has foreknown and predestined us from the foundation of the world (Romans 8:29–30). So, in his omniscience God knew exactly what Abraham would do before he tested him, since he knows all things (cf. Psalm 139:2–4; Jeremiah 17:10; Acts 1:24; Hebrews 4:13).

The Allegation That God's Repentance Implies He Does Not Know the Future

Neotheists also believe that God's repentance implies that he does not know the future. For if God had known in advance what humans would choose to do, then he would not have had to change his mind. Since we have already shown above that no Scriptures should be understood to state or imply that God actually changed his mind, we need not repeat the discussion here. The following issue does call for comment in this connection.

The Allegation That the Use of Anthropomorphism Is Illegitimate

Neotheists claim that interpreting texts that refer to God's "repentance" as metaphors is unacceptable. They insist that "we do not have to dismiss them as 'anthropomorphisms' or 'anthropopathisms,' which have no application to his real life." Rather, they believe "the open view of God does justice to a broad spectrum of biblical evidence and allows for a natural reading of the Bible" (OG, 49). The implied reason for rejecting these figures of speech is that it is not a "natural" interpretation of the text. But is this really the case?

In the very text that God is said to "regret" setting up Saul as king (1 Samuel 15:11, NKJV), God reveals himself as "the Glory of Israel [who] does not lie or change his mind" (15:29, NIV). In view of this, it could be argued that it would not be "natural" to interpret the reference to his "regret" (v. 11) in an anthropomorphic sense. In fact, it may be an anthropomorphism, since it expresses God's unchanging feeling or sorrow about Saul's sin.

Neotheists admit that the Bible often uses anthropomorphisms. As we have stated, the Bible often speaks of God having eyes, arms, legs, and even wings. And neotheists have no problem understanding these as anthropomorphisms. Why, then, could not God's alleged "repentance" also be an example of an anthropomorphism?

There is a kind of circularity about the neotheistic argument. On the one hand, they admit that in the same text it speaks of God as repenting and not repenting, thus making it necessary to interpret at least one of these instances as non-literal. And they do acknowledge the legitimate role of anthropomorphisms in the Bible. This being the case, how can they be sure that God's repenting must be taken as metaphorical and not literally? Are they using some criteria outside the text to determine how the text should be interpreted? Could it be they are presupposing their view of a changing God as the ground for knowing which should be taken literally?

All of this is not to say that it is illegitimate to take extrabiblical propositions as legitimate criteria for discovering the meaning of a text. One would assume that all rational beings would use the law of noncontradiction (which is an extrabiblical proposition) in deciding that when the Bible says God is "infinite" (Psalm 147:5, NKJV) and that he has "eyes" (Hebrews 4:13), he cannot have two or more infinite eyes in an infinite body. Likewise, when the Bible tells us that there are "four corners" of the earth (Revelation 7:1), would we not use the general revelation outside the Bible that the world is spherical to confirm that this is a figure of speech and not to be taken literally? So there is nothing wrong with bringing extrabiblical propositions to the text to help interpret it, provided we have good reason to believe they are true. But to claim that expressions like "God repented" can be shown not to be anthropomorphisms simply by looking at the text (rather than offering an independent exegetical argument for the so-called "open" view of God) may conceal a hidden philosophical commitment to a process view of God's nature.

Conclusion

This discussion by its very nature does not include all the attributes of God in question, or all the disputed verses used to support neotheism. It is, however, representative of the most significant ones. And the result of our analysis yields this conclusion: neotheism fails to establish a biblical basis for its beliefs. In fact, even one of the proponents admitted that they have not presented a compelling case when he wrote: "I do not consider our model to be logically superior to all others. . . . Nor do I believe the open model to be experientially superior. . . ." He goes on to say that he finds it only to be "the most plausible, appealing conceptualization of this relationship" (OG, 176).

As for being "plausible," we withhold comments until we have examined the theological and philosophical arguments (in the next two chapters). As for "appealing," this is scarcely an objective test for truth. Many theological errors, even heresies, have been appealing to a lot of people for a long time. Biblically, the neotheists have presented nothing that would lead one to forsake the venerable history of Christian interpretation supporting the classical theistic understanding.

CHAPTER FIVE

THE THEOLOGICAL CHARGES OF NEOTHEISM

In the previous chapter we discussed the biblical basis for neotheism. Here we will examine its theological coherency. Admittedly, the preceding "biblical" discussion has also been theological and philosophical. But this should not be surprising, since philosophy cannot be avoided in doing proper exegesis. Even the basic laws of thought and hermeneutics (without which the biblical text cannot even be interpreted) are philosophical issues, to say nothing of the worldview pre-understanding one brings to the text. The philosophical attack on the traditional view of God takes several forms.

The Charge That Theism Is Rooted in Greek Philosophy

One of the stock arguments against the classical view of a non-temporal, unchangeable God is that it has its origin in Greek philosophy. Take God's aseity as a case in point. The debate centers on the interpretation of Exodus 3:14. Neotheists contend that classical theists' understanding of the "I AM" as the self-existent God was really imported from the Greeks. The Jewish philosopher Philo, known for his platonic leanings, is said to have misinterpreted the verse this way. Later, Origen and the early church Fathers joined him (OG, 106).[1] Then Augustine, Anselm, and Aquinas followed suit. The Reformers largely left this classical view of God unchallenged. And unfortunately, neotheists argue, much of modern evangelicalism is infected with the same error. But it all began when "Philo understood Exodus 3:14 ... to mean: 'My nature is to be, not to be described by name'" (OG, 69). He is held responsible for passing on such ideas to classical theism (OG, 77).

Two points neotheists offer in support of their view are that (1) "Greek philosophers were looking for that which was stable and reliable in contrast to the earthly world of change. . . ." and (2) "This leads to the distinction between being and becoming or reality and appearances" (OG, 68). They insist that by the Greek translation of the Old Testament "the dynamic 'I AM' of the Hebrew text became the impersonal 'being who is there' of the Greek Septuagint (LXX), enabling theologians like Philo and Origen to link a changeless Greek deity with the God who acts in history" (OG, 106).

In response, several important observations need to be made. First, surely we are not to believe that the quest for something unchanging beneath all the flux of experience is necessarily bad. If so, this begs the question up front in favor of a process view of reality. Further, this impugns Hericlitus, the Greek "father of process philosophy" himself. For he believed that beneath all the flux of this world there was an unchanging Logos by which it could all be measured.

Second, it confuses the Greek quest for an unchanging metaphysical principle with their concept of God. But the Greeks never identified their ultimate metaphysical principle with God. This was the unique Judeo-Christian contribution to philosophy of religion.[2] Thus, the reverse of the traditional objection is the case. It was the Judeo-Christian concept of self-existent, pure actuality (based on Exodus 3:14) that transformed Greek metaphysics![3]

Moreover, the attempt to blame philosophy cuts both ways. One can equally argue that neotheistic reinterpretations of the biblical texts are influenced by contemporary process philosophy (see chapter 3). Indeed, the proponents admit that "process theology [to which they acknowledge some strong affinities (OG, 140)] itself is vulnerable to criticism for excessive deference to philosophy—in this case, to the process philosophy of Whitehead" (OG, 141). The same appears to be true of neotheism, which owes strong allegiance to process thought.

Furthermore, there is nothing wrong as such with having a philosophical influence on biblical and theological studies. Again, philosophy is necessary to do both exegesis and systematic theology. One need only be sure that he is utilizing good philosophy. Whether it is "platonic" or "process" is not the question, but rather whether it is *true*. Indeed, the proponents of neotheism correctly, but not self-critically, assert that "no one should criticize the Fathers for trying to integrate current philosophical beliefs and biblical insights. If the God of the universe and of truth is one, theologians should try to integrate all of the truth that they know from any quarter" (OG, 106).

The Charge That a God Who Acts in Time Is Temporal

Another reason put forward in support of the new theism is the argument that acting in time makes God temporal. This reasoning can be summarized this way: (1) God acts in time; (2) All acts in time are tainted by time (they have a before and an after); (3) Therefore, a God who acts in time is tainted by time (i.e., is temporal).

In response, it should be observed that there is confusion here between the eternal *Actor* (God) and his temporal *actions*. The neotheist assumes that the cause of any temporal act must itself be temporal. But no proof is offered that this must be the case. The argument given proves only that the *effect* is temporal, not the *cause*. Indeed, classical theists have gone to great lengths to demonstrate that the cause *cannot* be temporal like its effect—in both Kalam original-cause[4] and in the thomistic current-cause arguments.[5] The cause is eternal and the effect is temporal. Or, the cause is infinite and the effect is finite. So, there is absolutely no reason to suppose that the cause of an effect in time must be temporal as the effect is. By analogy, a logical inference is not temporal simply because it takes time to spell out the premises and conclusion in words.

Another way to state the problem is to note that process and neotheist thinkers who use this argument confuse God's *attributes* and his *acts*. His acts are in time, but his attributes are beyond time. There is no reason why the Eternal cannot act in the temporal world. Just as all the radii of a circle are many and yet the center from which they come is one, even so God can have multiple acts in a temporal sequence without being multiple himself. Likewise, just as spokes move faster at the circumference, and not at all at the absolute center, even so God's actions can occur in a moving temporal world without him moving through time. There is nothing logically incoherent about a timeless God acting in a temporal world.

What is interesting to note is that at times the proponents of the new theism come very close to recognizing this or a similar distinction when they claim that while God changes, nevertheless, his "essential nature" remains unchanged (OG, 28). What then is changing? At times they say it is his "will," and at other times they imply that it is part of his nature, albeit, a nonessential part. Since the former suggestion will be discussed later, the latter will be addressed here. If "part" of God's essence can change and another "part" cannot, then God is not an indivisible being. He must have at least two "parts" or poles, one that is changing and another that is unchanging. But this view is not theism but the heart of bipolar panentheism—the very thing the new theism disclaims. Or, to put the objection in another way, if God is necessary in his unchanging part (pole) and not necessary (i.e., contingent) in his changing part (pole), this raises a whole nest of metaphysical problems. Which attributes of God are necessary and which are not? How do we know which are which? How do we know God's moral attributes (love, purity, truthfulness, etc.) are part of his unchanging nature? Further, if God is contingent in one part, then this means he has the possibility not to be. (Only a necessary being has no possibility not to be.) But as Aristotle taught us, and good reasoning supports, no mere potentiality for existence can actualize itself. For it cannot be in a state of actuality and potentiality at the same time. In other words, the mere potentiality to exist cannot actualize anything. Only what actually exists can actualize a potential to exist.

The Charge That God's Knowledge of the Temporal World Makes Him Temporal

The neotheistic argument can be stated in this manner: (1) God knows temporal events; (2) The truth value of temporal events changes with time (e.g., Luther is not now tacking up his Ninety-Five Theses. He did this in A.D. 1517); (3) Hence, God cannot know temporal events without his knowledge changing.

But here again there seems to be a confusion of categories. An infinite, eternal God knows *what* we know but not in the *way* we know it. As an eternal being, God knows eternally. As temporal beings, we know temporally. Each being must know in the way he can know, namely in accordance with his own nature. For instance, neotheists believe that God is infinite. If so, then he must know infinitely. But we are finite and know only finitely. Therefore, God knows what we know only in a different way than we know it.

Further, neotheists believe in *ex nihilo* creation, so they must admit that at least before creation God was eternal and knew eternally. This is logically necessary, since time had not yet been created, and God cannot be an eternal number of moments.[6] So, even the logic of the neotheistic position demands that God must know in a different way than we know.

The Charge That Statements Cannot Be Made About a Nontemporal God

According to the new theistic way of reasoning, no references from our temporal perspective can be made to a nontemporal being. For: (1) All statements made by a temporal being are temporal; (2) God is nontemporal; (3) Therefore, none of our statements about God can really apply to him. In short, agnosticism about God would follow from claiming that he is nontemporal.

In response, several important things should be observed. First of all, since neotheists believe that God is infinite and necessary, then by the same logic we could argue that: (1) All of our statements about God are finite (and contingent); (2) God is not finite (i.e., infinite) and not contingent (i.e., necessary); (3) Therefore, none of our statements about an infinite and necessary God (which neotheists claim to hold) can really apply to him. Since neotheists are not willing to admit this, they must redraw this argument against a nontemporal God. For all our statements about God are as conditioned with contingency and finitude as they are with temporality.

Further, it does not follow that temporal (contingent, etc.) beings cannot make true statements about a nontemporal (non-contingent, etc.) God. What the neotheist fails to see is that this is not really an argument against God's non-temporality but rather an argument for the analogous use of religious language. Of course, temporal statements cannot be applied to God *univocally*, that is, in the same way they are applied to temporal things. If they could, God would have to be nontemporal. But this begs the question in favor of univocal predication about God. If statements about God are *analogous*, there is no problem. For an analogous statement is both similar and different. And the difference is that God cannot be whatever he is (loving, holy, just, etc.) in a temporal, contingent, finite way. He must be eternal, necessary, and infinite love, holiness, and justice.

Unless the neotheist is willing to accept the total (self-defeating) agnostic view that "no statements can be applied to an eternal God (including this statement)," then we must accept some form of analogy. This is precisely what classical theists like Aquinas did, arguing that all finite and limited conditions must be negated of a term before it is applied to God.[7] If some statements (such as neotheists hold) can be applied to God, then they can be only because they first remove from them all finite conditions. For example, if God is "uncreated," all conditions of createdness must be removed from the term before it can be appropriately applied to God. The same is true of God as "uncaused," "ontologically independent," and "infinite"—all of which neotheists believe.

The Charge That Creation of a Temporal World Implies a Temporal Creator

Unlike panentheism, neotheism maintains that "the triune God is Creator of the world out of nothing. This means that God does not simply influence preexisting matter but that everything depends on God for its existence." And, "It also implies that God has the power to intervene in the world, interrupting (if need be) the normal causal sequences" (OG, 109). But if God can act in time, argue neotheists, God must be temporal. For whatever acts in the temporal world is part of the temporal process. And the temporal process involves a past, present, and future. So that when God acted in bringing Israel from Egypt there was a time before that and a time after that redemptive act. Thus God is tainted with time by the very fact that he acts in time.

In reply, we simply point out that there is a difference between saying God created *in* time (as neotheists claim) and that he is the Creator *of* time (as theists affirm). There was no time before God made the temporal world. Time began with the world. God "framed the ages" (Hebrews 1:2; cf. John 17:5). So God was *ontologically* prior to time but not *chronologically* prior. That is, he was prior in being to his creation but not in time. Consequently, there is no problem of how God could create a world in time without being temporal himself. There was no temporal continuum before he created the world that would make it necessary for him to choose a moment in time to create. Rather, from all eternity God chose to create the temporal continuum itself, which has a beginning.

It is also worthy of note here that it is equally incoherent to speak of God as being eternal before creation and temporal after creation. For creating the world did not change the nature of God. The act of creating did not transform the Creator into a creature. The world was not created *ex Deo* (out of God); that is pantheism. To the theist, the world was created *ex nihilo* (out of nothing). So, God did not change "internally" (that is, in his essence) by creating something else. The only thing that changed is "external," namely, his relationship with the world. Prior to creation God had no relationship to a created world, because there was none to which he could relate. At creation and after, God was properly called a Creator. (It was not appropriate to be called a Creator until he created something.) Prior to creation he was God but not Creator. That is, God gained a new *relationship* but not any new *attributes*. He did not change in his *essence* but in his external *activity*. There is no change in what God *is* but in what he *does*. Failure to make this distinction leads to the neotheistic confusion of speaking of God changing in his nonessential nature.

Further, the neotheist makes the same errors that were noted earlier. He assumes that to act in time is to be temporal. He does not demonstrate that the *Actor* is temporal; only that his *acts* are. Classical theists do not deny that God's *actions* are temporal. They only insist that God's *attributes* are not temporal. God cannot have a nonessential nature. "Nonessential" means God has something in himself that he does not need to have. But "nature" is what is essential to a thing. For example, human nature is essential to humans. Without it we would not be human. So a nonessential nature in God is a contradiction in terms. Because nature means essence, it would be a nonessential essence, which is essentially nonsense.

To state the point another way, neotheists recognize there is a difference between an uncreated Creator and a created world. One has no beginning and the other does. One has no temporal starting point and the other does. In this same way, classical theists insist that God is beyond time, even though he made time. This should not be difficult to understand. After all, every Creator is beyond his creation—the way an artist is beyond his painting or a composer is beyond his composition.

The Charge That the Incarnation Implies God Is Temporal

The Bible declares that Jesus is God, and that he entered this temporal world (John 1:1, 14). Neotheists claim that by simple logic it would seem to follow that in Christ, God lived a temporal life. To deny this would appear to be a denial of the deity of Christ Incarnate. They point to this as proof that God is a temporal being.

Now admittedly this argument seems stronger than the previous argument from creation, since a Creator is beyond his creation, but here the Creator "became" part of his creation. Hence, it would appear that the Incarnation of God in human flesh is indeed proof that God, at least in Christ, became a temporal being. In point of fact, the premises seem to be true (according to orthodox Christianity), and the conclusion is validly drawn from them. (1) God became human in the Incarnation of Christ; (2) Human beings are by nature temporal beings; (3) Therefore, God became by nature a temporal being in the Incarnation.

Although this is a valid conclusion, it is false because the first premise is untrue. It is based on an unorthodox assumption, namely, that it was the divine nature that became human in the incarnation. Nor was it the human nature that became divine, thus leaving only one divine nature. As a matter of fact, this is a form of the Monophysite heresy condemned at the Council of Chalcedon in A.D. 454. It is a confusion of the two natures of Christ. In the Incarnation the divine *nature* did not become a human nature or vice versa. Rather, the divine *person*—the second person of the Trinity—became man. Notice carefully the words of Scripture. "The Word was God. . . . And the *Word* was made flesh, and dwelt among us" (John 1:1, 14, KJV). It does not say that *God* became flesh. It is as impossible for God to become man as it is for an infinite to become a finite or an uncreated to become created. As Athanasius would say, in the Incarnation it was not the substraction of deity but the addition of humanity. God the Son did not change his divine nature. Rather, he added a distinctly different human nature to it. So, whatever apparent plausibility the neotheist's argument possesses is based on unorthodoxy. Once one rejects the Monophysite-like error, this argument against God's immutability fails.

The Charge of Fallacy Against the "Perfect Being" Argument

Proponents of "open" theism also reject classical theism because of what they call "the difficulties of a perfect being theology" (OG, 132). "If God were to change, so the argument goes, then he would change either for the better or for the worse. But God cannot change for the better, since he is already perfect. And he cannot change for the worse, for this would mean that he would no longer be perfect. So God cannot change" (OG, 131).

The proponents of neotheism reject this argument, not because God is not perfect but because "it rests on the assumption that all change is either for the better or for the worse, an assumption that is simply false" (OG, 132). They offer the "immutable watch" as an example. It registers the same time day in and day out. By contrast, an "extremely accurate watch" always registers the correct time, even though it is constantly changing. However, when it changes, its change is not for the better or worse. It remains the same in its changes, namely, an extremely accurate watch.

Remembering William Paley's fate, one hesitates to get involved with another watch analogy, but this one seems to contain a significant category mistake, namely, comparing a changing being with an unchanging Being. The illustration shows how one changing thing (the clock) is not better when it changes to another changing thing (time). But this begs the question in favor of a nonimmutable view of God. The illustration does not tick if one assumes that God does not change, for in that case anything that represented him as changing would be inaccurate as it changed. Or, to put it another way, they assume (not prove) that God is temporal and changing (like time). Hence, in order for something to keep "perfect" time it has to change. But this begs the question by assuming (per the illustration) that God is changing. If God is not temporal as theists argue (see chapter 2), then what changed would not thereby correspond to him perfectly.

Further, even the neotheistic critique here implies that God does not really change. For they assert that whatever changes there are in God are "consistent with and/or required by a *constant state of excellence*" (OG, 133, emphasis mine). But what is this "constant state of excellence" but an unchanging nature? And if it is, then neotheism here depends on the classical theist's view of God, which it rejects.

Furthermore, their response reveals an underlying premise that God does not really change in his essence. They speak of the possibility of an unchanging God suffering from "imperfection" (OG, 132), if a worshiper became disappointed with worshiping a God who could not change. But how could one know God was *im*perfect unless he presupposed an absolute, unchanging standard of perfection (which theists claim God is)? Here again, it appears that the only way to make sense out of neotheism is to assume theism is true.

Finally, even if one were to grant the theist's argument on perfection, it is not the only argument for immutability in the theist's arsenal. (1) The numerous, clear, and emphatic biblical declarations that God cannot change (Psalm 102:25–27; Hebrews 1:11–13; 6:18; Titus 1:2; Malachi 3:6; 1 Samuel 15:29; Numbers 23:19). Neotheists give only passing and incomplete reference to and no serious analysis of the many verses supporting the unchangeableness of God (OG, 47). (2) There is the argument from God's pure actuality. For any change implies the being that changed had the potential to change, but a God of pure actuality has no potentiality. There are also other arguments that support God's unchangeability (see chapter 2).

The Charge That an Unchangeable God Is Unrelatable to a Changing World

Another objection given by neotheists (which, like most of their other philosophical arguments, comes from panentheists) is that an eternal, immutable God cannot have a real relationship with a changing world. The essence of the argument is this: (1) All real relationships involve change; (2) An unchanging God cannot change; (3) An unchanging God cannot have a real relationship with a changing world.

As noted earlier, Aquinas anticipated this objection and treated it extensively and adequately. First, he argued that there is a real relationship between the unchanging God and the changing world.[8]

However, since creatures are dependent on God, but God is not dependent on them, they are actually related to an idea. That is, God *knows* about the relationship of dependence but he does not *have* it. Only the creature has ontological dependence. Thus, when there is a change in the creature there is no change in God. Just as when one changes his position from one side of the pillar to the other, the pillar does not change; only the person changes in relation to the pillar. So, while the relationship between God and creatures is real, God is in no sense dependent in that relationship.

It is important to note here that the theist is only denying a *dependent* relationship and not all *real* ones. He is denying that God changes in his relationship with the world but not that there are no real changes in his relation with the world. The person's relation to the pillar really changes when he moves, but the pillar does not change. And when that happens, then the pillar no longer has this relationship with the person. The neotheists should not have difficulty grasping this, since they believe in *ex nihilo* creation in which God was not related to the world before it was created, but he was after. Yet they believe that both before and after creation God is independent of the world. If so, then God can be really related to the world while not changing in that he is independent of it even when its relationship to him changes. So, it is a real relationship of dependence on the part of the creatures, but there is not a relation of dependence on the part of God (see chapter 2).

The Charge That a Loving God Must Be Changeable

Neotheists labor hard the point that God is love. Ironically, while clear statements about God not changing (listed above) are not taken literally, neotheists have no difficulty viewing "God is love" as unquestionably literal. They confidently affirm: "The statement *God is love* is as close as the Bible comes to giving us a definition of the divine reality" (OG, 18). Again, "Love is the essence of the divine reality, the basic source from which *all* of God's attributes arise" (OG, 21).

Their argument for the necessity of change in a God of love goes like this: (1) God is essentially love; (2) Love of necessity involves the possibility of change; (3) Therefore, God's love necessarily involves the possibility of change.

The crucial second premise is supported by a raft of material roped together to show that God's love is a dynamic, interactive activity whereby God engages in a give-and-take relationship with his creatures. Love suffers with the loved one (OG, 46), and therefore God cannot be impassable as traditional theism affirms. Indeed, the Cross is the prime example of the sympathetic, suffering, and changing love of God. Leech is quoted with approval saying, "The Cross is a rejection of the apathetic God, the God who is incapable of suffering, and an assertion of the passionate God, the God in whose heart there is pain, the crucified God" (OG, 46).

At the very start one notices something strange about this argument against God's unchangeableness—the very first premise begins with a God who cannot change. For God is "essentially" love. But if God by his very nature is love and cannot be otherwise, then God cannot change in nature. Indeed, neotheists admit the same when they affirm that "God's essential nature and his ultimate purpose did not change" (OG, 28). But is the premise that "God cannot change in his essential nature as love" consistent with their conclusion from this premise that God must be able to change *because* he is love?

Further, the second premise appears to be a classic example of the quip that *God made man in his own image, and man returned the compliment!* Who says God has to love the same way we love? To be sure, human love is changing because human beings are changing beings. Theism affirms that God is an unchanging being and, therefore, he must love in an unchanging way. God can do whatever good we can do, but he does not do it in the *way* we do it. He does it in an infinitely better way than we do—an unchanging way. Even neotheists admit that God is infinite, ontologically independent, uncreated, and transcendent. But even granting that God is infinite demands that he is and does things differently than finite beings do. The same is true of other attributes that neothesim admits God has.

The Charge That Foreknowledge of Free Acts Entails Determinism

So-called "free will theists" claim that God is "omniscient." But they hasten to qualify God's omniscience so that he cannot know what future free choices will be. God knows for sure only what he determines. But future free acts are as yet undetermined. Hence, they cannot be known by God.

In short, God can know whatever is knowable. But future free acts are not knowable. Consequently, God is not fully omniscient in the classical sense.

The argument can also be stated this way: "If God knows already what will happen in the future, then God's knowing this is part of the past and is now fixed, impossible to change." And "since God is infallible, it is completely impossible that things will turn out differently than God expects them to." But "if God knows that a person is going to perform it, then it is impossible that the person fail to perform it—so one does not have a free choice whether or not to perform it" (OG, 147).

In responding to this view, we note up front that neotheists admit not only that this is a diversion from the historic theistic position but that it is influenced by process theology. William Hasker wrote: "It will no doubt have been noticed that the conclusions we have reached agree, on an important point, with the conception of God's knowledge developed in process theology."[9]

Further, in response to this argument one need only quote from one of the greatest classical theists of all time, Thomas Aquinas: "Everything known by God must necessarily be" is true if it refers to the statement of the truth of God's knowledge, but it is false if it refers to the necessity of the contingent events.[10] Since God is an omniscient being, he knows with *certainty* what we will do *freely*. The fact that he knows "in advance" from a temporal perspective does not mean the event cannot happen freely. For God can know *for sure* that the event will occur *freely*. The necessity of his knowledge about the contingent event does not make the event necessary (i.e., contrary to free choice). It simply makes his knowledge of this free event an infallible knowledge.

The Claim That a Proper View of Free Will Demands That God Can Change

Neotheists challenge the theistic contention that God's will cannot be changed. They insist the Bible speaks of God repenting (changing his mind) and, furthermore, good reason supports the fact that God is open to change. Indeed, they believe that a proper view of free will (which God has) demands that he be able to change. This is true of free creatures made in God's image, and it is true of the God in whose image they are made. Indeed, the very attributes of God as loving, compassionate, and merciful imply that he can change.

Any adequate reply to this argument must point out that it is a gigantic category mistake. It simply does not follow that because free will in the creature implies they change their mind that it must also entail this in the Creator. There are many attributes possessed by the Creator that the creature does not have. Neotheists believe that God is uncreated, necessary, and infinite. Yet creatures are none of these. Further, there are many things even a neotheistic God cannot will. He cannot will to cease being God. He cannot will to go out of existence. He cannot will to be a creature. He cannot will to sin. Indeed, the Bible declares that "it is impossible for God to lie" (Hebrews 6:18).

Furthermore, if God is omniscient (see following page), then he knows what will be. But what he knows will be, will be. That is, what God knows will come to pass, will come to pass. God's will is in perfect accord with his knowledge. Hence, God literally cannot change his mind, for if he did it would mean that his mind (knowledge) had changed. Therefore, God's will is as unchangeable as his mind.

This does not mean God does not will that some things change. It means that God's will does not change, even though he does will that other things change.[11] Of course, the Bible speaks of God repenting. But God repents only in a metaphorical sense, as man views it. Actually, God knew from eternity if people would repent. And God's will includes intermediate causes such as human free choice. So God knows what the intermediate causes will choose to do. And God's will is in accord with his unchangeable knowledge. Therefore, God's will never changes, since he wills what he knows will happen. That is to say, what is willed by conditional necessity does not violate human freedom, since what is willed is conditioned on their freely choosing it. God wills the salvation of men only conditionally. Therefore, God's will to salvation does not violate human free choice; it utilizes it.

Of course, while God's will does not change, its effects in time do change. For God wills unchangeably from all eternity that many different and changing things will happen at different times so that eventually his sovereign will is accomplished. Just as a doctor knows and wills in advance to change the patient's medicine when their condition changes, even so God wills unchangeably from all eternity to meet the changing conditions of his creatures in order to accomplish his ultimate purposes. An omniscient Mind cannot be wrong about what it knows. Again, therefore, the statement "Everything known by God must necessarily be" is true if it refers to the state of God's knowledge, but it is false if it refers to the necessity of the contingent events (see chapter 2).

The Charge That God Cannot Have Unlimited Omniscience

Neotheism also rejects the classical concept of omniscience in favor of a limited form of omniscience.[12] In principle omniscience is defined the same; namely, that God can know anything that is possible to know. "However," neotheists hasten to add, "omniscience need not mean exhaustive foreknowledge of all future events." Why? Because "total foreknowledge of the future would imply a fixity of events. Nothing in the future would need to be decided." Further, it also would imply that human freedom is an illusion, that we make no difference and are not responsible" (OG, 121). But in actual fact neotheists hold that God cannot know future free acts. Thus, they believe in a limited omniscience. The evidence given for this includes a number of things. Since the biblical evidence has already been weighed and found wanting, we will treat the chief theological arguments here.

First, it is claimed by some that God can only know what is real, not what is unreal. And the future is not real. So, God cannot know the future. But the future *is* real. Reality is comprised of both the actual and the potential. Potentialities are real. For instance, there is a real difference between the potential of dry wood, which can burn at normal fireplace temperatures, and wet wood, which does not have this potential. Likewise, humans have the potential to learn calculus, and laboratory rats do not. There is a real difference between the potential of steel to be made into an automobile and the potential of water for the same purpose. But if potentials are real, and the future is a potential that has not yet been actualized, then there is no reason why a mind that can know whatever is real cannot know the future.

Other neotheists narrow the argument this way: God can know only what is possible. It is not possible for him to know the future. Therefore, God cannot know the future. Certainly the classical theist need not disagree with the form of this argument. But he would emphatically disagree with its content. For the traditional theist insists that by definition an omniscient (all-knowing) being knows everything that is possible to know. And the only thing that is impossible to know is an impossibility (e.g., an actual contradiction like a square circle). But the future is not an actual contradiction, otherwise it would not be able to materialize like it does. Therefore, it does not follow that God cannot know the future.

At this point the neotheist must bring forth some evidence that shows why there are some aspects about the future that even an all-knowing God cannot know. This they often do by way of the free will argument, which affirms that God cannot know future free acts without determining them. But if God determines them, they are not really free. Even granting (what extreme Calvinists are not willing to grant) that God cannot force any free act (since forced freedom is a contradiction), the neotheistic argument against full omniscience does not follow. For there is a big difference, on the one hand, between determining the future by omniscient foreknowledge of how people will use their freedom and, on the other hand, of determining the future by forcing people to do things against their free choice. The theist's response can be spelled out in several premises.

God Knows the Potential As Well As the Actual

Aquinas argued that God's knowledge is not simply of the actual; he also knows the potential. He knows both what is and what could be. He knows what *will* be and what *can* be. For God can know whatever is real in any way it can be known. And both the actual and the potential are real. Only the impossible has no reality. Thus, whatever is potential is real. This being the case, it follows that God can know what is potential as well as what is actual.[13] This means that God can know future contingents, that is, things that are dependent on free choice. For the future is a potential that preexists in God. And God knows whatever exists in himself as the cause of those things.[14] So, God does not have to wait to see what will happen. He knows it eternally in his eternal mind. Hence, his knowledge is not dependent on it happening (as Molinists claim). A totally independent being cannot be dependent on anything. And since God's knowledge is one with his eternal and independent mind, it follows that God knows everything that will yet be (to us) within his eternal and unchangeable essence.

God Knows Timelessly

Furthermore, if God is a timeless being, then he knows all of time in one eternal now. But the future is part of time. Therefore, God would know the future, including the free acts to be performed in it. So the problem of not knowing future free acts is inherent in a temporal view of God but not in a non-temporal view. God sees (in his eternal present) the whole of time: past, present, and future (for us). But if God sees our future in his present, then our future is present to him in his eternity. In this way there is no problem as to how he can *fore*see free acts. He does not need to *fore*see; he simply *sees*. And what he sees (in his eternal now) includes what free acts will be performed in our future.

The Charge That Infallible Knowledge Would Eliminate Free Choice

Of course, whatever God knows is known infallibly, since God cannot err in his knowledge. And since a theistic God knows future contingents, it follows that they too would be known infallibly by him. According to neotheism, this would mean there are no true free acts, since God has determined everything in advance. In brief, a classical theist's view of God eliminates true (libertarian) free acts.

The basic reply of classical theism includes two important observations. First, this objection confuses two things, for free actions are contingent with regard to their immediate cause (human free choice) but necessary with regard to God's knowledge. Second, it fails to note that God can know free acts without causally determining them. For an omniscient being can know whatever is not impossible to know. And, as we have just seen, it is not impossible for a timeless being to know all of time in one eternal now. God simply sees (in his now) with certainty what free creatures do freely, including what is in our future.[15]

So here again there is no demonstrable incoherence in classical theism. Conversely, it is neotheism that is inconsistent, since it borrows many premises from classical theism that are contrary to its own beliefs.

Conclusion

In summation, the theological charges of neotheism against classical theism fall short of the mark. Thus, they have not proven the need to discard this venerable tradition from the early Fathers through the Reformers and into contemporary evangelicalism. The weight of both history and theology favors classical theism. There is no proven need for innovation. Indeed, the evidence is to the contrary. Furthermore, as we shall see in the next chapters, there is an inherent danger in the very creation of this new view. Both philosophical and practical problems in neotheism are the subject of the next two chapters.

CHAPTER SIX

THE PHILOSOPHICAL COHERENCY OF NEOTHEISM

Ironically, while neotheism rejects certain attributes of God held by classical theism (see chapters 4–5), certain other attributes of God embraced by neotheism lead logically to the very attributes of God they reject in classical theism. Other attributes of the neotheistic God are compatible with panentheism (see chapter 3), a view they reject as such. Thus, there is a basic incoherence within neotheism that leaves it in a logically vulnerable position. One thing seems certain. Neotheists cannot have it both ways. Logically, they cannot be a half-way house between theism and neotheism. They must choose to go one way or the other.

For example, if God is really the transcendent uncreated Creator *ex nihilo* of the space-time universe, then other attributes of traditional theism (such as eternality, pure actuality, and immutability) follow logically. If, on the other hand, God is temporal and changing in his essence, as neotheism claims, then he must be limited, bipolar, and spatial just as panentheists hold. But logically neotheism cannot have it both ways.

Certain Neotheistic Beliefs Entail Classical Theism, Not Neotheism

First, we will consider how classical theism follows from certain neotheistic beliefs about God. This is evident from their affirmation of *ex nihilo* creation.

God's Eternality Follows From Creation Ex Nihilo

Neotheism affirms that God created the entire spatio-temporal universe (see chapter 2). But if this is so, then time is part of the essence of the cosmos. In short, God created time. But if time is of the essence of creation, then it cannot be an attribute of the uncreated—that is, of God who is beyond time and the Creator of it. The Creator of time cannot be temporal, since time has a beginning and its Creator does not. For the principle of causality demands that everything that has a beginning (or comes to be) had a cause. The universe and time had a beginning. Hence, it must have a cause (i.e., God) who did not have a cause. This being the case, God is not part of the temporal order any more than the Creator is part of the creation; or, the infinite God is part of the finite world he made. Therefore, God must be the nontemporal Cause of the temporal world. The attribute of nontemporality is exactly what neotheists reject, yet it appears to follow logically from their own view of creation. So if neotheists would be consistent with their own position, they should accept classical theism's view of the nontemporality (eternality) of God.

If neotheists attempt to avoid this conclusion by holding that somehow time existed before creation, then further problems emerge, both scientific and logical. First of all, according to the dominant contemporary scientific understanding, both time and space are correlative. It is the space-time universe. There is no time without space and no space without time. If so, then the logical consequence of affirming that God is temporal would be to assert that he is also spatial. This falls right into the lap of process theology (see chapter 3), which neotheists claim to reject.

Second, there are also logical problems with affirming that God is temporal. This would mean that time is either inside God, that is, part of his nature, or else outside God. If inside, then how can God be without a beginning, since an infinite number of temporal moments appears to be incoherent (as proponents of the Kalam argument for God's existence have shown)?[1] For if there were an infinite number of moments before today, then today would never have come (since an infinite cannot be traversed). But today has come. Therefore, there were not an infinite number of moments before today but only a finite number. That is, time had a beginning. But if God were temporal, then he would have had a beginning. This leads to the legitimate question: Who made God? For whatever has a beginning or comes to be (but not necessarily what is eternal) had a cause. Subsequently, the neotheistic view leads to a God who needs a cause and, hence, is not really God at all, that is, the Ultimate Cause. But such a being by definition is not God. And, further, the ultimate beginningless cause of this God who needs a cause would really be God, since he alone is uncaused and beginningless. And this leads right back where the neotheist does not wish to go, namely, to a nontemporal cause of the universe. In short, the neotheistic belief in the creation of the spatio-temporal universe leads logically to classical theism.

If, on the other hand, neotheism claims that time is "outside" God, then some sort of dualism emerges. For, if time is outside God, then we must ask whether time had a beginning or not. If it did not, then it could be argued that there is something outside God that he did not create, since it is as eternal as he is. And this is no longer theism in either the classical or neotheistic sense. In fact, it is a form of dualism where some reality eternally exists outside God that was not created by him. On the other hand, if time is outside of God and had a beginning, then it must have been created by God (since everything with a beginning had a cause). And in this event we are right back to the theistic position that time is created by God, and that God, as the Creator of time, is not temporal.

God's Transcendence Implies His Nontemporality

According to neotheism, God is beyond creation. He is more than and other than the entire spatio-temporal world. But, again, if God is beyond time (i.e., the temporal), then he cannot be temporal. The neotheist might reply that God is also immanent in the temporal world. And whatever is immanent in the temporal is temporal. However, a proper theistic understanding of God's immanence does not make him *part* of the world (as in pantheism) but only *present* in the world (as in theism). God is in the world in accordance with his being, and his being is nontemporal. So, he is in it in a nontemporal way. For example, God is a necessary being. And yet he is immanent in the contingent world. But this does not make him contingent. Rather, as even neotheists admit, God the necessary being is immanent in the contingent being in accordance with his being, which is necessary. As Creator he is immanent in his creation. So, immanence of a nontemporal God in a temporal world does not demand that God is temporal. Again, what neotheism affirms about God leads logically to the view of classical theism, which it rejects.

Necessity Implies Pure Actuality

The classical theistic view of God also follows from the neotheist's belief that God is a necessary being. For if God is a necessary being, then he cannot *not* be. That is, God has no potential in his being *not* to be. But if God has no potentiality in his being, then he is pure actuality. So the classical theistic view of God follows from what neotheists admit about God's necessity. But they reject the attribute of pure actuality. Thus, neotheism is inconsistent and incoherent. Logically, if God is a necessary being, then he must also be pure actuality. He cannot be the former without being the latter.

God's Uncausality Implies His Pure Actuality

The new theism also believes that God is an uncaused being. But it denies he is a God of pure actuality, as traditional theism claims. For the God of neotheism is the cause of all other beings but is himself not caused by any other being. That is, God is uncaused. But if God is uncaused in his being, then he must be pure actuality. For whatever is not caused never came to be. For to be caused to exist means to have one's potential to exist actualized. But what has no actualized potential has no potential to be actualized. As a result, an uncaused being must have been pure actuality.

Thus, the neotheist's belief that God is an uncaused being logically entails what they say they reject, namely, that God is a being of pure actuality with no potentiality in his being. Here too, a crucial neotheistic belief leads logically to classical theism. But, ironically, that is precisely what neotheism rejects. Thus, neotheism has no firm, logical ground on which to stand, for it holds some attributes of God that logically entail other attributes that they explicitly reject. In short, there is a serious incoherence in neotheism.

Certain Neotheistic Beliefs About God Lead to Panentheism

Not only do some of the attributes of a neotheistic God logically imply classical theism, which it rejects, but others entail panentheism, which it also claims is false. For instance, if God is temporal and changing in his essence, as neotheism claims, then he must be limited, bipolar, and spatial just as panentheists claim. But logically neotheism cannot have it both ways.

God's Temporality Logically Leads to His Being Created

According to neotheism, God is a temporal being; he is in time. But a temporal being experiences one moment after another. And such a temporal chain of moments cannot be eternal, as the proponents of the Kalam argument for God's existence have shown.

In view of the disastrous logical consequences of concluding that God is temporal, it would be better for neotheists to discard their concept of God being in time. However, once they do this they have accepted the nontemporal view of God, which they claim to have rejected in classical theism. Yet the alternatives appear to be stark: either classical theism is true or else God, like everything else that is temporal, had a beginning.

When faced with such dilemmas, neotheists tend to make exceptions for God: He alone has a special kind of temporality. For one thing, God alone is beginningless time. But as we have seen, actual beginningless time appears to be incoherent. For everything that involves one moment after another before the present is finite, since it is impossible to cover an infinite number of actual moments. In any such series of *actual* moments there could always be one more, and so on. Of course, *abstract* infinite numbers are possible. But they are only *conceptual*, not *real* (concrete). For example, there are an infinite number of *abstract* (dimensionless) points between the ends on my bookshelf, but I cannot get an infinite number of *actual* books between them no matter how thin the books are! This being the case, it is futile to appeal to God as being beginningless time. Even the great skeptic David Hume agreed with this conclusion, insisting that "an infinite number of real parts of time, passing in succession and exhausted one after another, appears so evident a contradiction that no man, one should think, whose judgment is not corrupted, instead of being improved by the sciences, would ever be able to admit it."[2]

Other neotheists, sensing the problem, speak of God as being the Creator and Lord of time. But this maneuver is fruitless as well. For these phrases either imply that God is qualitatively different from time or else he is not. If the former, then God is really eternal (nontemporal) as classical theism claims. In this case, neotheism collapses into classical theism on this point. If, on the other hand, God is not qualitatively different than time, then he must have had a beginning too. And we are right back to the previous criticism.

To focus the point, consider what it means to be "Creator" of time. It means that time had a beginning and the Creator did not. It means the Creator was ontologically prior to time (in his being). That is, he existed in an eternal state where there was no time, no succession of moment after moment. But this is precisely what classical theism means by eternal or nontemporal. This should not be difficult to understand. For even neotheists admit that God is different from the temporal world. For example, God is not material (i.e., is immaterial); God is not contingent (i.e., is necessary); God is not spatial (i.e., is immense); God has no beginning (is beginningless). Yet the world is all of these. Why then cannot God be nontemporal, even though the world is temporal? In fact, God must be nontemporal, since temporality had a beginning. And neotheism contends that God does not have a beginning. God cannot be temporal because he existed before there was any such thing as temporality.

Some have suggested that God was eternal before he created a temporal world and temporal after he did. But this makes no more sense than saying that God was Creator before he created and a creature after he created. God does not cease being God when he creates. He does not cease being the uncaused Cause when he causes. It makes sense to say that God was not *related* to the world before he made it and was related to it after he did. But a change in *relationship* does not necessitate a change in *nature*. God remains nontemporal in his nature after he creates a temporal world just as he remains infinite in nature after he created a finite world.

God's Temporality Implies Finitude

Neotheism affirms with theism that God is infinite or unlimited in his nature. They also insist that God is temporal, subject to time. But here again they cannot have both. For to be temporal necessarily implies limitations. As was shown above, a temporal being is limited in duration. That is, it cannot be eternal. So, temporality implies finitude. Thus here again neotheism logically reduces to panentheism or process theology (the God of neoliberalism).

The dilemma is this: if God is infinite, he is not temporal. If he is temporal, then he cannot be infinite. This is definitely true of God's duration. And it is also true of his nature. For either it is of the nature of God to be temporal or it is not. If it is of the nature of God to be temporal, then God is by nature a succession of moments. But, as we have seen, such a series is limited. As a result, a temporal God is limited by his very nature. If the neotheist replies that time is not part of the nature of God but is "outside" of him, a created thing, then his view affirms classical theism. For this is exactly what is meant by God being nontemporal and beyond time. Here again neotheism is on unstable ground. Logically it comes down to either theism on the one hand or panentheism on the other. If God is really infinite, then he cannot be temporal. And if he is really temporal, then he cannot be infinite. Neotheism cannot have a God who is both infinite and temporal.

God's Temporality Entails God Being Spatial

Another problem for neotheism arises out of the concept of God as a temporal being. For if God is temporal, then he must also be spatial, since space and time are held to be correlative. As mentioned earlier, contemporary science speaks of the space-time universe, i.e., there is no time without space and no space without time. If this is true, then logically a temporal world would also be spatial. And since what is in the space-time universe is also material, it would follow that God would also be material. While such a concept is not repugnant for process theology (which holds that the universe is God's "body"), it is emphatically rejected by biblical theism. For the Bible declares that "God is spirit" (John 4:24) and "a spirit does not have flesh and

bones" (Luke 24:39). Therefore, if neotheism wishes to remain biblical and not become another form of process theology, it would
appear they must give up the concept of God being temporal in his
being. In short, they must return to classical theism.

A Denial of God's Pure Actuality Implies God Is Bipolar

According to neotheism, God is not pure actuality as classical theists claim. This concept of God being pure being, they claim, is derived from Greek philosophy and not from the Bible (see chapter 4).
However, neotheists do not seem to draw the full implication of such
a claim. If God is not pure actuality but has some unactualized potential, then God has two poles—an actual one and a potential one.
But this is precisely what panentheism holds. Yet neotheists insist
they are not panentheists, that is, bipolar theists (see chapter 3).
However, if God is not pure actuality with no unactualized potential,
then he must have both actuality (since he actually exists) and potentiality (since not everything in him is actualized). And these two
dimensions of God are different—the actual is not the potential and
the potential is not the actual. But if God has two dimensions or
poles, then he is bipolar and not monopolar—the very thing panentheists believe. Here again, given certain things neotheists believe
about God, their view logically reduces to panentheism (process theology).

Affirming That God Can Change Leads to Bipolar Theism

According to neotheism, in contrast to classical theism, God can
change. By this they do not simply mean that God engages in changing actions or activities. Rather, God can change in his very nature,
though not in his unvarying purposes. Yet some neotheists speak of
a deep dimension of God, in which his unchanging purposes are
rooted, which does not change (see chapter 3). But if there is a part
of God that does change and a part that does not, then God must
have at least two aspects or poles to his makeup. Here again, we are
right back to a form of bipolar theism or process theology, which
neotheists claim they reject. However, logically it appears to be un-

avoidable. For if there is in God's very being a dimension that changes and one that does not, then he is two-dimensional, not one-dimensional. He is bipolar (having two poles), not monopolar (with only one pole). But this is a crucial difference between classical theism and process theology. And once again, neotheism by logical reduction comes out on the wrong side.

Claiming God Is Not Simple Implies Multiple Polarity

Along this same line, neotheists attack the traditional attribute of simplicity (indivisibility) in God. They insist that an absolutely simple being cannot engage in multiple activity. For God's nature, they assert, is tainted by his actions. But granting that God is not absolutely simple, we must conclude that God has multiple aspects to his being. He is multipolar. Further, if God is not indivisible, then he must be divisible. But whatever is divisible is destructible, at least insofar as it is divisible.[3] Hence, denying God's indivisibility would appear to lead logically to a denial of his indestructibility. It is not only risky to "fool Mother Nature," as the figure of speech goes, but it is even more dangerous to tamper with God's nature!

Conclusion

There are serious logical flaws within neotheism. On the one hand, it affirms in common with classical theism certain attributes and activities of God (such as transcendence, uncausality, necessity, and creation *ex nihilo*). But each of these logically entails some attribute of God that neotheism rejects. In point of fact, they lead to classical theism, which neotheism labors to avoid. On the other hand, neotheism denies certain attributes of God (such as nontemporality, unchangeability, and pure actuality). Significantly, the affirmation of temporality, changeability, and potentiality in God leads logically to a process, bipolar theism, which neotheists claim they wish to avoid. But logically they cannot have it both ways. Both classical theism and panentheism are self-contained models in which the basic attributes stand or fall together. Therefore, if one accepts some of them, the rest come with the package, whether they are wanted or not.

Neotheism finds itself in a theological no-man's-land. For confessedly it fits neither into the categories of classical theism nor contemporary panentheism—deserving a category of its own. Nonetheless, it desires to partake of mutually exclusive attributes, some from classical theism and others from contemporary panentheism. But since these are internally consistent but mutually exclusive systems, one cannot pick and choose among God's essential attributes. This leaves neotheism with an internal incoherence and makes it logically self-destructive and predictably short-lived. Logically, they cannot have it both ways. They must decide which God they will serve—the God of Augustine, Anselm, Aquinas, and the Reformers or the God of Whitehead, Hartshorne, Ogden, and the process theologians.

CHAPTER SEVEN

THE PRACTICAL CONSEQUENCES OF NEOTHEISM

But what difference does it make? Is not all this discussion about theism and neotheism simply a matter over which scholars debate? Aren't we really just talking about how many angels can dance on the head of a pin? Does it really make any difference in our Christian life? Yes it does; beliefs do make a difference in our behavior. Doctrine does affect our deeds. And even if it seems very theoretical, we must remember that a good theory is a very practical thing.

Ideas do have consequences. Good ideas have good consequences. And bad ideas have bad consequences. If a person really believes his life is threatened by an intruder in the night, he may shoot in self-defense only to find he has killed his sleepwalking teenager! If a skater actually believes the ice is safe when it is not, then he may break through and drown! To embrace false teaching, especially about God, is to skate on thin ice. It is dangerous to our spiritual well-being.

We have already spoken (in chapters 4–6) of the biblical, philosophical, and theological difficulties with neotheism. We now turn our attention to some serious practical consequences on Christian belief and practice.

If Neotheism Is True, Predictive Prophecy Is Fallible

If neotheism is true, then we cannot trust the Bible as the infallible Word of God. For neotheists believe that God does not have an infallible knowledge of future free acts. God knows only future events that are a result of a necessary chain of events. But nearly all, if not all, future events in the world involving human beings are the result of free acts somewhere along the way. This means that no events resulting from free choice could be known infallibly in advance by God. Yet in the Bible, God made many predictions about the future. It would follow that either all of these biblical prophecies are fallible, or else they are purely conditional and not really predictive.

However, the Bible declares that God is omniscient. He knows all things, including the future. Indeed, God makes unconditional predictions about the future, even of events that involve human free will. There are numerous specific predictions in the Bible. These include that Cyrus would be king of Persia (Isaiah 45:1); the destruction of Tyre (Ezekiel 26:3–14); the doom of Edom (Petra) (Jeremiah 49:16–17); the course of the world's great kingdoms (Daniel 2, 7); the closing of the Golden Gate (Ezekiel 44:2); the exact city in which Christ would be born (Micah 5:2); the time he would die (Daniel 9); the return of Israel to the Land (Isaiah 11:11); the increase of knowledge and transportation (Daniel 12:4); and many more events (see Appendix A). But such unfailing predictions are not possible apart from a Mind that has infallible knowledge of the future, including free acts.

Not only were the above predictions given without condition and fulfilled without fail, but some promises of God about future events are stated as specifically and emphatically unconditional. For example, he made unconditional predictions about the physical descendants of Abraham living in the land of Canaan forever (Genesis 13:15; 15:18–21; 17:7–8). And the apostle Paul, when speaking of the future of the nation of Israel, insisted that "God's gifts and his call are irrevocable" (Romans 11:29). So these predictions have never been revoked. That they have not been fulfilled in some spiritual sense in the Christian church is evident from the fact that in Romans 11 Paul is speaking of literal national Israel whom he had previously identified as his "kinsman according to the flesh" (Romans 9:3, KJV) and that this Israel will yet be restored (Romans 11:17–26).

The logical and practical consequence of believing that God's omniscience is limited to events not resulting from human free actions is that we cannot have complete confidence in God's ability to predict these kinds of future events. And since human free actions are intertwined with all future human events, it follows that if neotheism is right, then we lose confidence in God's ability to guarantee our future.

It is important to notice that this consequence affects the Arminians as well as the Calvinists. For God cannot even predict with certainty that an Arminian will be saved based on his free choice, since God does not know what future acts of apostasy they may yet commit. Indeed, God cannot know for sure who will make it to heaven and who will not. This means that God cannot choose the elect, whether based on his own purposes (as Calvinists claim) or based on his foreknowledge of who will believe (as many Arminians believe). In short, both classical Arminianism and Calvinism are destroyed by neotheism!

If Neotheism Is True, the Bible Is Not Infallible

Strangely, some neotheists, such as Clark Pinnock, claim to believe in the infallibility and inerrancy of the Bible. However, this is clearly inconsistent. Other neotheists insist that only a Calvinist can consistently be an inerrantist. As two neotheists argued, the Bible cannot be inerrant unless one holds the Calvinist view of free will, which they reject.[1] They argue that inerrancy holds that the Bible cannot err. But the neotheistic view of freedom (libertarian) insists that since the Bible was written by free creatures it can err. Hence, the Bible could be in error.

Likewise, other neotheists insist that if some predictions in the Bible are fallible, then the Bible is not infallible, at least not in these areas. And, according to neotheism, all predictions involving human free choice are fallible. Thus, it follows that the Bible (which makes many such predictions) cannot be a completely infallible book. On the contrary, since the Bible is an infallible book, then it would follow (by their own logic) that neotheism is false.

What Saith the Lord?

The denial of the infallibility and inerrancy of the Bible runs contrary to the Bible's claim for itself. Jesus said, "I tell you the truth, until heaven and earth disappear, not the smallest letter, not the least stroke of a pen, will by any means disappear from the Law until everything is accomplished" (Matthew 5:18). Indeed, he declared that "the Scripture cannot be broken" (John 10:35). In brief, the Bible is the Word of God (Matthew 15:6; Mark 7:13; John 10:35), and God cannot err (Romans 3:4; Titus 1:2; Hebrews 6:18). Therefore, the Bible cannot err. A more extended defense of inerrancy will be found elsewhere.[2] It suffices to note here that for a neotheist to claim both the inerrancy of Scripture and the fallibility of God's foreknowledge is inconsistent. Neotheism leads logically to the denial of inerrancy. The only way a neotheist can claim to believe in inerrancy is to be inconsistent. One cannot help but wonder why, then, some neotheists claim both.

How Then Shall We Live?

There is a nagging practical problem for the Bible-believing Christian, namely, when should he trust the Bible and when should he not trust it? How can we know when the Bible makes a prediction involving a free act whether or not what God said is true? For if all such prophecies are conditional, how can we be sure they will come to pass? Even if the Bible affirms that something is true and that it will come to pass, it may be in error if such pronouncements are not infallible. Indeed, on the premise that God is only guessing about the future (and, thus, hedging his bet with a conditional promise), it is reasonable to assume that some of these guesses *are* wrong. It would be begging the issue to assume that it just so happens that all of his guesses will turn out to be right.

Two ways to avoid this conclusion is to claim (1) that not all predictions involve free choice, or (2) that God overpowers free choice on those occasions he desires his plan to be accomplished. However, neither of these two alternatives is really consistent with the position of free will theism.

All Human Events Involve Free Choices

All, or nearly all, human events involve free choice, either directly or indirectly. Mary and Joseph chose to go from Nazareth to Bethlehem (Luke 2:1–7). Yet it was predicted hundreds of years earlier that it would be this small city in Judah in which the Messiah would be born (Micah 5:2). The same is true of the name and existence of the tribe of Judah, which the Old Testament predicted would be the one from which Christ would come (Genesis 49:10). It would seem that virtually all predictive prophecy involves free choice in some way. Micah's prediction that the Messiah would be born in Bethlehem involved the free choice of his parents to be there, even though they lived elsewhere (in Nazareth) at the time (cf. Luke 2:4).

Indeed, the Bible predicted when he would die (Daniel 9:25–27), how he would die (Isaiah 53), and that he would rise from the dead (Psalm 16:10; cf. Acts 2:30–31). In order for these to be fulfilled, there had to be an incredible web of free activity, including Jesus, his disciples, and even his enemies. Yet the Bible predicted that these events would occur, and they did. Also, if God does not know future free acts for certain, then he does not know that the beast and false prophet will be in the lake of fire. But the Bible says they will be there (Revelation 20:10). Hence, either this prophecy could be false or else neotheism is not correct. If all human events involve free choice, then God cannot know any future human event infallibly without tampering with free choice. And if this is so, then no prediction in the Bible is infallible and unconditional. Ultimately, no free will theists can consistently hold to the complete infallibility and inerrancy of the Bible. In this respect they are inconsistent. For logically their position on prophecy is a denial of the infallibility and inerrancy of the Bible.

Before leaving prophecy, another point must be addressed. Neotheists claim that "the problem with the traditional view on this point is that there is no *if* from God's perspective. If God knows the future exhaustively, then conditional prophecies lose their integrity" (OG, 52). But this is a confusion of two perspectives. Of course, from God's perspective (since he knows the future infallibly) every thing is certain. But as noted above, this does not mean that from the human standpoint these actions are not chosen freely. It is simply that God knew for *certain* how they would *freely* exercise their choice (see chapters 4–5).

Overpowering Free Choice Is Contrary to Freedom

Neotheists are aware of the above criticism and respond by making a significant, and systemically destructive, exception. They argue that since God is omnipotent he can, and sometimes does, overpower human freedom in order to accomplish his ultimate goal. As a result, some predictions can be made infallibly because God can and will accomplish them even if he has to override human free choices to do so. This exception, however, proves to be fatal to the neotheist's system for two reasons.

First, if God can and does overpower free choice on *some* occasions to accomplish his foreordained purposes, he could do so on *all* occasions. If that is true, neotheists have already admitted *in principle* the truth of the view they vehemently reject, namely, the strong determinist's position that the future is predetermined by God, even if he must overpower free choice to do so. If a neotheist wanted to maintain his or her free will distinctive consistently (that God never overpowers free choice), it would seem there would be a better way to explain the data. All they would have to do is acknowledge, as classical theists do (see chapter 2), that God can infallibly know future free acts without causally determining them, that is, without forcing the choices to be made. Indeed, as was shown earlier, there is no demonstrated incoherency in this position if God is an eternal being and is not really *fore*seeing free acts but only *seeing* them in his eternal now. And if, as traditional theists say, all effects preexist in their Cause, then knowing the future infallibly is no more difficult than God knowing himself (see chapter 2).

Second, and more pointedly, free will theism leads logically to some form of annihilationism or universalism. For if God can and sometimes does override freedom to accomplish his saving purposes, why doesn't he do it all the time? The strong Calvinist has a ready answer to this: God is under no obligation to do so. He can choose to save none, some, or all. By his grace, he chose to save some. The rest are justly condemned. But neotheists are Arminian and they do not accept the premise that there is nothing in God that prompts him to love and attempt to save all. They believe, as does this author, that "God so loved the world . . ." (John 3:16), and he is "not wanting anyone to perish" (2 Peter 3:9) but "wants all men to be saved"

(1 Timothy 2:4). If all were automatically saved, this would lead logically to universalism (see p. 143).

Of course, the remaining alternative is annihilationism. Instead of sending anyone to hell, God could simply snuff them out of existence. But this would be the harshest form of violation of free choice—the very thing neotheists detest. They may avoid the strong Calvinist view, but annihilationism is worse, since it not only violates one's freedom, it obliterates it! (see p. 144).

If Neotheism Is True, the Test of a False Prophet Fails

Moses declared in the Law that "If what a prophet proclaims in the name of the LORD does not take place or come true, that is a message the LORD has not spoken. That prophet has spoken presumptuously. Do not be afraid of him" (Deuteronomy 18:22). That is, a false prophecy is a sign of a false prophet.

But neotheism claims that all prophecy is conditional; none is infallible. Even prophecies that come from God can be wrong. If this were so, there could not be any such thing as a false prophecy. But the Old Testament lays down specific tests for false prophets, one of which is whether or not the prediction comes to pass. For, again, "If what a prophet proclaims in the name of the LORD does not take place or come true, that is a message the LORD has not spoken. That prophet has spoken presumptuously" (Deuteronomy 18:22). If the neotheists are correct, this test is not valid. But if it is valid (since God gave it), then neotheism is not true.

True Prophets and False Prophecies

If neotheism is right, then even things uttered by true prophets in the Bible could be false. For much, if not all, of what they wrote was interwoven with future free acts, which God (according to neotheists) cannot know for sure. Thus, we are faced with the specter of a true prophet, even Moses who was confirmed by acts of God (Exodus 4:1f.; cf. Isaiah 44:25–26), who can utter a false prophecy. Furthermore, it would render the use of miracles as a divine confirmation of God's truth to be ineffective (John 3:2; Acts 2:22; Hebrews

2:3–4; 2 Corinthians 12:12). For even an alleged revelation of God, confirmed by an act of God, could be false. This not only undermines an apologetic for Christianity but also any credibility in prophetic claims on which the Bible is based. These are serious and disastrous consequences of neotheism. The price is too high to pay for the alleged benefits (see chapters 4–5).

Will the True Prophet Please Stand Up?

If neotheism is correct, there is no real test here for a false prophet. For the fact that a prophecy is false does not necessarily mean it was given by a false prophet. It may mean that God, being limited in his omniscience to only necessary events (but not free ones) could not foresee for sure what would happen. As Frank Beckwith noted, "The limited omniscience position is inconsistent with the biblical test for a prophet, for when they are juxtaposed the following conclusion is drawn: God is not God. But this is absurd."[3]

If neotheism is true, the test for a false prophet given in Deuteronomy is a false test. It does not work, since it does not really distinguish a false prophet from a true prophet. Indeed, even a prophet confirmed by miraculous acts of God could be giving a false prophecy. Here again, this would undermine the biblical apologetic which, in the case of the crucial doctrine of the resurrection of Christ, was said to be based on "many infallible [indisputable] proofs" (Acts 1:3, KJV). Of what value, then, is this test for a false prophet? Indeed, logically we must conclude that God erred when he gave this test to Moses (Deuteronomy 18:22).

Let God Be True—Most of the Time

The Bible proclaims that "it is impossible for God to lie" (Hebrews 6:18). Indeed, Paul said, "Let God be true, and every man a liar" (Romans 3:4). But according to neotheism, God's predictions involving free acts are only guesses, no matter how good they are. If neotheists are correct, this text should be modified to read "Let God be true—most of the time!" Perish the thought! It approaches blasphemy to even suggest that the God of all truth, whose word cannot pass away (Matthew 5:17–18), could utter a falsehood at any time.

Did God Really Say?

If neotheism is right, then one thing is certain: nothing involving free creatures is absolutely certain—even if God says it. For beneath every word of Scripture involving human free choice, there is the implied doubt of Satan's hiss: "Did God really say. . . ?" (Genesis 3:1). Could we ever be sure when reading Scripture that God has any more than unerring intentions clothed in undetectable errors? How would we really know what is true and what is not? The truth is that we would not—that is, if the neotheist is right.

Neotheism Destroys the Apologetic Argument From Predictive Prophecy

One of the strongholds of the Christian defense of the faith has also been the unique supernatural nature of predictive prophecy. As Bernard Ramm put it in his classic book *Protestant Christian Evidences*, the argument from prophecy is the argument *from* omniscience. It is the argument that "limited human beings know the future only if it is told them by an omniscient Being."[4] And the Bible has made numerous and specific predictions that have been literally fulfilled. There are some 191 biblical prophecies with reference to Christ.[5] These include:

1. Genesis 3:15: *Born of a Woman* (Galatians 4:4; cf. Matthew 1 and Luke 2);
2. Genesis 12:1–3: *The Seed of Abraham* (Matthew 1:1; Galatians 3:16);
3. Genesis 49:10: *The Tribe of Judah* (Luke 3:23, 33–34; cf. Matthew 1:1–3; Hebrews 7:14);
4. 2 Samuel 7:5–8: *The House of David* (Matthew 1:1; 21:9);
5. Micah 5:2: *Born in the City of Bethlehem* (Matthew 2:1–6);
6. Isaiah 40:3: *Heralded by the Messenger of the Lord* (cf. Matthew 3:1–3);
7. Isaiah 11:2: *Anointed by the Holy Spirit* (Matthew 3:16–17);
8. Isaiah 61:1–2: *Messiah's Ministry to Preach the Gospel* (cf. Luke 4:17–19);
9. Isaiah 35:5–6: *Would Perform Miracles* (cf. Matthew 9:35; Matthew 11:4–5);

10. Malachi 3:1: *The Cleansing of the Temple* (John 2:12–17);
11. Psalm 118:22: *Rejected by the Jewish People* (cf. 1 Peter 2:7; cf. Matthew 21:42; Mark 12:10; Luke 20:17; Acts 4:11);
12. Isaiah 53:2–12: *Suffering and Death of Christ* (cf. Matthew 26–27; Mark 15; Luke 22–23; John 18–19). There are at least twelve things mentioned in Isaiah's prophecy including his being: (a) rejected by men; (b) a man of sorrows; (c) life of suffering; (d) despised by others; (e) carried our sorrow; (f) smitten by God; (g) pierced for our transgressions; (h) wounded for our sins; (i) suffered like a lamb; (j) died with the wicked; (k) was sinless; (l) prayed for others.
13. Daniel 9:24–27: *The Time of Christ's Death*: Speaking of 445/444 B.C. (the time the command was issued under Artaxerxes in Nehemiah 2) "to restore and rebuild Jerusalem" (Daniel 9:25)—not the earlier command by Cyrus (536 B.C.) to return and build the "house of the Lord" (Ezra 1:3), Daniel predicted that it would be 483 years to the time of Christ's death. Taking the commonly accepted date of A.D. 33 for the crucifixion[6], this would give us 483 years exactly. For 444+33=477. Adding six more years to make up the other five days in a solar year, not in a lunar year (5 days×477=2385 days or 6+ years. And 477 + 6=483 years).[7]
14. Psalm 16:10: *Christ's Resurrection* (Acts 2:30–31; cf. Acts 13:35).
15. Psalm 110:1: *The Ascension of Christ* (Ephesians 4:8; Matthew 22:43–44; Acts 2:34–36).

Many biblical prophecies do not relate directly to the Messiah, but they are specific and predictive nonetheless. They support the supernatural nature of the Bible. They include Daniel's prediction of the great world kingdoms (Daniel 2:37–45); the existence and activity of Cyrus, the king of Persia, by name over one hundred years before he was born (Isaiah 44:28); the return of exiled Israel to their land after a nearly 2000-year exile (Isaiah 11:11); the increase of knowledge in the last days (Daniel 12:4), and many more (see Appendix One). Even if there were only one such prediction involving free choice in the Bible (and there are many), it would falsify the neotheist's claim that God cannot foresee such events without violating the free choice of the humans involved.

The Neotheistic God Cannot Guarantee Ultimate Victory Over Evil

If, as neotheists insist, God does not know the future for sure and does not intervene against freedom except on rare occasions, then it seems to follow that there is no guarantee of ultimate victory over evil. For how can he be sure that anyone will be saved without fettering freedom, which contradicts the neotheist's libertarian view of free will?

And, as noted above, positing the annihilation of all who choose evil does not solve the neotheist's dilemma. For this is the ultimate violation of free choice—the total destruction of it! This is to say nothing of the fact that both Scripture (Luke 16; Revelation 19:20; 20:10) and centuries-old orthodox Christian teaching stand against this aberrant view.

It is also contrary to the Bible, which predicts that Satan will be defeated, evil will be vanquished, and many will be saved (Revelation 21–22). But since, according to the neotheist, this is a moral question that involves (libertarian) free will, it follows that God could not know this infallibly. If this is so, then neither God nor the Bible can be completely infallible and inerrant, though some neotheists claim that they are. This is patently inconsistent.

Neotheism Undermines God's Unconditional Promises

It is clear that not all God's promises in the Bible are for everyone. Some are only to certain individuals (Genesis 4:15). Others are only to a certain group of people (Genesis 13:14–17). Some are only for a limited time (Joshua 1:5). Many promises are conditioned on human behavior. They have a stated or implied "if" in them. The Mosaic covenant is of this type. God said to Israel, "Now *if you obey me* fully and keep my covenant, then out of all nations you will be my treasured possession" (Exodus 19:5–6, emphasis added). Other promises, however, are unconditional. Such was the land promise to Abraham and his offspring. This is clear from the facts that (1) No conditions were attached to it; (2) Abraham's agreement was not solicited; (3) It was initiated while Abraham was in a deep sleep (Genesis 15:12); (4) The covenant was enacted unilaterally by God who passed through the split sacrifice (Genesis 15:17–20); (5) God re-affirmed this promise even when Israel was unfaithful (2 Chronicles 21:8). Now such unconditional promises, which involve the free choices of creatures, would not be possible unless God at least knows all future free choices.

Neotheists offer 1 Kings 2:1–4 as an example of how a seemingly unconditional promise is really conditional. God promised David concerning his son Solomon: "My love will never be taken from him, as I took it from Saul, whom I removed from before you" (2 Samuel 7:15). Yet later God seemed to take this back, making it conditional on whether he would "walk faithfully before me" (1 Kings 2:1–4). Thus, they argue that all seemingly unconditional promises are really conditional.

However, this argument fails for many reasons. First of all, it is a non sequitur (does not follow), since their conclusion is much broader than the premises. Even if this instance were an example of an implied conditional, it would not mean that all promises are con-ditional.

Second, it overlooks the many cases in Scripture (see above) where there are unconditional promises. These provide counter-examples that refute the contention that all God's promises are con-ditional (cf. 2 Timothy 2:13; Romans 9:16; 11:29).

Third, it is inconsistent with the neotheists' own view, for they insist that God is an ontologically independent being. But God's knowledge is part of his essence or being. How then can God's knowl-edge be dependent on anything else?[8]

Finally, the argument is based on a failure to see that the two texts refer to two different things. Second Samuel was speaking to David about never taking the kingdom away from his son Solomon. This promise was fulfilled, for in spite of his sins (1 Kings 11:1–2), the kingdom was not taken from Solomon during his entire life-time. In fact, the fulfillment was explicitly stated when God said to Solomon: "Since this is your attitude and you have not kept my covenant and my decrees, which I commanded you, I will most cer-tainly tear the kingdom away from you and give it to one of your subordinates. Nevertheless, for the sake of David your father, *I will not do it during your lifetime.* I will tear it out of the hand of your son" (1 Kings 11:11–12). So God did keep his promise to David about Solomon.

The other text (1 Kings 2:1–4) is not speaking about God's promise to David about his son Solomon. Rather, it refers to God taking the kingdom from any of Solomon's sons. There was no unconditional promise made here. From his deathbed David exhorted Solomon: "Walk in his [God's] ways, and keep his decrees and commands . . . that you may prosper in all you do and wherever you go, and that the LORD may keep his promise to me: '*If your descendants* watch how they live, and *if* they walk faithfully before me with all their heart and soul, you will never fail to have a man on the throne of Israel' " (1 Kings 2:3–4). This promise was both conditional ("if") and limited to Solomon's sons. It said nothing about Solomon, concerning whom God apparently made an unconditional promise not to take his throne away during his lifetime.

One of the consequences of making all predictions conditional is that it undermines confidence in God's promises. If we cannot be sure that God can keep his word, our belief in his faithfulness is seriously threatened. But the Bible says we can accept God's Word unconditionally. Sometimes it says this explicitly in the context of affirming that he makes known "the end from the beginning" (Isaiah 46:10). In this context Paul wrote, "If we are faithless, he will remain faithful, for he cannot disown himself" (2 Timothy 2:13). Again, he reminds us that "God's gifts and his call are irrevocable" (Romans 11:29). Consequently, with regard to these unconditional promises, "It does not, therefore, depend on man's desire or effort, but on God's mercy" (Romans 9:16).

If Neotheism Is True, We Have No Assurance of Salvation

One of the practical consequences of neotheism for the Christian life is that there is no real assurance of salvation. This not only means, in traditional terms, there is no eternal security, but neither is there any present assurance for an Arminian who is not living in sin. In short, if neotheism is true, then both traditional Arminianism and Calvinism, in either strong or moderate forms, must be rejected.

But there is good biblical evidence that at least what these views have in common is true. For example, the Bible declares that a certain group (generally called the "elect") will eventually be in heaven. Paul affirmed that "for those God foreknew he also predestined to be conformed to the likeness of his Son, that he might be the first-born among many brothers. And those he predestined, he also called; those he called, he also justified; those he justified, he also glorified" (Romans 8:29–30). For the Arminian this means that all whom God knew would endure to the end would be saved, and God knew exactly who these would be. For the Calvinist it means that God will guarantee by his effectual grace that everyone whom he regenerates will eventually be in heaven, that is, they will endure to the end. But whether a person is an Arminian or a Calvinist, one of the logical and practical consequences of neotheism is that there can be no assurance in this life that he or she will ultimately be saved, even if they are not living in sin. For God himself does not know who is going to make it until the very end because he cannot foresee what they will do with their free will. Thus, he cannot provide them with the assurance of salvation now or at any time—even if they are not living in sin!

Neotheism Undermines Our Confidence in God's Ability to Answer Prayer

In spite of the fact that neotheists make much of God's dynamic ability to answer prayer, it would appear that their concept of God actually undermines God's use of special providence in answering prayer. They admit, as indeed they must, that most answers to prayer do not involve a direct supernatural intervention in the world. Rather, God works through special providence in unusual ways to accomplish unusual things. But a God who does not know for sure what any future free act will be is severely limited in his logistic ability to do things that a God who knows every decision that will be made can do. So, ironically, the neotheistic view of God is a liability to answered prayer, which they consider so important to a personal God.

Neotheism Implies That God Does Not Know Who Will Be in Heaven

If neotheism is correct, God does not know who will be in heaven until they get there. In traditional terms, God does not even know who the elect are! They opt for a corporate election, in which God knows that Christ is elect and, therefore, all who are in him will be elect—whoever they are. But there are serious objections with this view. For the Bible tells us that there will be *some* elect, but according to neotheists, God cannot even be sure there will be *any* elect. The "bus" destined for heaven may be empty of any occupants who freely chose to take it.

Furthermore, how can they even be certain that any bus is going to heaven? After all, according to their view, before Christ lived they could not even be sure that Christ would choose to resist evil (for presumably he has a libertarian free will too). No wonder one process theologian, after whom neotheism's view on this is patterned, said that God is waiting with bated breath to see how things will turn out!

This conclusion is contrary to the Bible. For Scripture informs us that Christ was the lamb slain from the foundation of the world (Revelation 13:8, KJV) and that some elect were chosen in him before the creation of the world (Romans 8:29; Ephesians 1:4). Finally, Paul includes himself among those whom God knew and chose before the foundation of the world (Ephesians 1:4, KJV). But if God cannot know future free acts, then this would not have been possible.

Neotheism Leads Logically to Universalism

Christian neotheists are unequivocally committed to God's omnibenevolence. They believe that God loved all, Christ died for all, and God desires to save all (1 Timothy 2:4; 2 Peter 3:9). But they also believe that God could save all, even if some were unwilling, since he is omnipotent and can override their will if necessary. The question is whether all these premises can be held consistently. It would seem not. For if it is morally right for God to intervene sometimes against free will to guarantee his ultimate desire to provide salvation for mankind, then why not all the time? This exception undermines the whole neotheistic position and leads to universalism. For if it is right for God to violate freedom on some occasions for our salvation, then why not on all occasions? After all, neotheists believe that God desires all persons to be saved. He is omnibenevolent. But if God is omnibenevolent and omnipotent and can (and sometimes does) override human free choice for salvific (salvation) purposes, then there is no reason he should not always do so. In brief, universalism seems to follow logically from neotheism. This is to say nothing of the fact that orthodox Christianity has consistently condemned universalism as heretical, and Christian neotheists have to this point generally shrunk back from this conclusion. Instead, many have opted for annihilationism. But this seems to fare no better under logical scrutiny.

Neotheism Negates Impetus to Missions

If in the end no one is going to be lost, then the question naturally arises, "Why send missionaries?" Of course, there is always the response that Christ commanded it. But why the urgency if they can and will be saved regardless? There is no question that the belief that everyone is eventually going to be saved (universalism) or at least that no one will suffer conscious separation from God forever (annihilationism) has a devastating effect on Christian missions. In fact, wherein is the real urgency to go to the ends of the earth to rescue the perishing if they are not really perishing? If they are not going to hell if they do not hear, then in the end our going or not going doesn't make any difference as to their eternal destiny. In this crucial sense, neotheism has a devastating effect on the motivation for missions and the salvation of the lost.

Annihilationism and Neotheism Are Inconsistent

In spite of the fact that they make exceptions, neotheists abhor violent acts against free choice. God works persuasively but not coercively, they insist. Even overpowering free acts to keep God's redemptive plan going is done sparingly. And when God does this, at worst, he is only temporarily suspending free choice, not permanently destroying it.

But annihilation is the most violent and permanent of all divine actions against a free creature. It destroys his free will forever! It is hard to conceive what could be more inconsistent with the free will theist's beliefs in God's omnibenevolence and libertarian free choice than annihilationism.

Conclusion

A person's view of God is the most important thing about which he thinks. A true view of God has good consequences. And a false view of God has disastrous consequences. Neotheism is a classic case in point. Springing out of the background of classical theism with strong influence from panentheism (process theology), neotheists are zealous in their desire to reform historic theism. But the consequences of neotheism are both many and dangerous.

Logically, neotheism leads to a denial of the infallibility of the Bible, the full omniscience of God, the apologetic value of prophecy, and a biblical test for false prophets. It also undermines confidence in the promises of God, his ability to answer prayer, and any ultimate victory over sin. Indeed, it leads logically to universalism and/or annihilationism. And even an alleged revelation of God, confirmed by an act of God, could be false. This undermines any apologetic for Christianity and any credibility in prophetic claims on which the Bible is based. These are the grave consequences of accepting neotheism—a very high price to pay for any alleged benefits (see chapters 4–5).

Despite protests to the contrary, neotheism leads logically to a form of process theology in which God has two poles, is changing, limited, and not in sovereign control of the world. In short, it has disastrous theological and practical consequences for evangelical Christianity.

INFALLIBLE PREDICTIONS THAT FALSIFY NEOTHEISM

Neotheism claims that God cannot make infallible predictions of future events that involve free actions. But virtually all human events involve free actions. Certainly the following examples do. Hence, if these predictions prove to be infallible, then they would falsify neotheism. There are many reasons that, taken together, show convincingly that the Bible makes infallible predictions. First, there are numerous predictions of this kind in the Bible. Second, they are specific in nature so as to ensure they were really predicted and fulfilled. Third, there are no known failures of any such predictions in the Bible. But repeated, specific, and unfailing predictions are evidence of infallibe foreknowledge.

Isaiah 44:28; 45:1 predicted Cyrus to be king of Persia some 150 years before Cyrus was even born. Isaiah lived between about 740 and 690 B.C., and Cyrus made his proclamation for Israel to return from exile about 536 B.C. (Ezra 1). The attempt of critics to make two Isaiahs and post-date the prophecy is without foundation and is a backhanded compliment to the definiteness and accuracy of the prediction. The evidence for one eighth century B.C. Isaiah who wrote the whole book is strong: (1) The book as a whole claims to be written by one and the same Isaiah (1:1; 7:3; 20:2, etc.); (2) Ancient Jewish teaching is attributed to this same early Isaiah (cf. Ecclesiasticus 48:17–25); (3) The same literary style, thoughts, phrases, and even figures of speech run throughout the book (cf. "Holy One of Israel"); (4) The details of the book are Palestinian and Jerusalem centered (cf. 45:22), which fit with the earlier period and not Assyrian-centered, which would fit with the later period; (5) There is no historical reference to any prophet Isaiah who lived in the later period; (6) The earliest manuscripts of Isaiah from the Dead Sea Scrolls show no evidence of two books being put together; it is one manuscript; (7) Jesus cited both sections of Isaiah and attributed them to one and the same prophet (cf. John 12:38–40).

Isaiah 11:11 (cf. Deuteronomy 28:1f.) predicted the Return of Israel to the Land. Given their long exile of some nineteen centuries and the animosity of the occupants of the land against them, any prediction of their return, restoration, and rebuilding as a nation was extremely unlikely. Amazingly, just as the Bible foretold, they were reestablished as a nation in 1948, and millions have returned and rebuilt their country and retaken their ancient capital. No other nation on earth has been totally destroyed, exiled for nearly two millennia, and then reestablished on their ancient land with their ancient language.

Ezekiel 44:2 predicted the closing of the Golden Gate. This is the eastern gate of Jerusalem, the one through which Christ made his triumphal entry on Palm Sunday before his crucifixion (Matthew 21). Ezekiel predicted that it would be closed until the Messiah returns. In 1543 Sultan Suleiman the Magnificent closed the gate and walled it up just as Ezekiel had predicted. He had no idea he was fulfilling prophecy but simply sealed it up because the road leading to it was no longer used for traffic. It remains sealed to this day exactly as the Bible predicted, waiting to be reopened when the King returns.

Ezekiel 26:3–14 predicted the destruction of Tyre. This was unlikely, since Tyre was an important sea port in the eastern Mediterranean and was one of the great cities of the ancient world. It was a heavily fortified and flourishing city. Yet the prophet Ezekiel predicted her doom a couple hundred years in advance, declaring: "Therefore this is what the Sovereign LORD says: I am against you, O Tyre, and I will bring many nations against you, like the sea casting up its waves. They will destroy the walls of Tyre and pull down her towers; I will scrape away her rubble and make her a bare rock. Out in the sea she will become a place to spread fishnets. . . ." This prediction was partially fulfilled when Nebuchadnezzar destroyed the city and left it in ruin. However, the stones, dust, and timber had not been thrown into the sea. More than two centuries rolled by before Alexander the Great attacked the seemingly impregnable island by taking the stones, dust, and timber from the ruined mainland city and building a causeway to it. Not only has the city never been rebuilt as the prophecy said, but today it is a place "to spread fishnets" (v. 5). This prediction was not only centuries in advance of the events, but it has been fulfilled in incredible detail—indicating infallible foreknowledge.

Jeremiah 49:16–17 prophesied the doom of Edom (Petra). Unlike many Old Testament predictions of doom, Edom was not promised any restoration, but "perpetual desolation." Jeremiah wrote: " 'The terror you inspire and the pride of your heart have deceived you, you who live in the clefts of the rocks, who occupy the heights of the hill. Though you build your nest as high as the eagle's, from there I will bring you down,' declares the LORD." Amazingly, this is precisely the condition of the country today, after two and a half millenia. Given the virtually impregnable nature of the city carved out of rocks and protected by a narrow passageway, this is an incredible prediction. Yet, just as Jeremiah said, in A.D. 636 it was conquered by Muslims and stands deserted but for tourists and passersby.

Ezekiel 36:33–35 predicted the flourishing of the desert in Palestine. This too was unlikely, since Palestine lay waste and desolate for centuries. Today roads have been built, the land is being cultivated, and it is flourishing just as Ezekiel had predicted.

Daniel 2, 7 predicted the course of human history. In the sixth century Daniel accurately and amazingly predicted the course of human history, one world kingdom after another, right up to our time. He predicted that Babylon would be followed by a kingdom known to us as Medo-Persia, then Greece, and finally Rome. He even predicted in detail regarding the second century B.C. Antiochus Epiphanes (Daniel 11). So accurate was Daniel that critics have labored in vain to post-date Daniel after these events. These efforts have failed because: (1) Daniel is known from Ezekiel (14:14, 20) to have lived in the sixth century B.C.; (2) The book reflects a careful and specific knowledge of the sixth century B.C.; (3) The ancient Jewish Talmud confirms that Daniel wrote it in the sixth century B.C.; (4) A careful comparison of the linguistic style and vocabulary of Daniel with that of the second century B.C. reveals that Daniel was from the earlier period; (5) Jesus referred to Daniel as a prophet (not a historian), noting his prediction about the destruction of Jerusalem that was yet future in Jesus' day and which came to pass in A.D. 70 (Matthew

24:15); (6) Even if it was written in the second century B.C., nonetheless, it predicted Christ's death some 200 years in advance to the very year (Daniel 9). And if he could make such a precise supernatural prediction here (Daniel 9), then there is no reason that he could not make them elsewhere (like Daniel 2, 7).

Daniel 12:4 predicted the increase of knowledge and communication in the last days. He said, "Many will go here and there to increase knowledge." Never in the history of the world has there been a greater burst in knowledge, transportation, and communication than in our time. The jet airplane and computer have caused a transportation and information explosion that is only beginning to boggle the mind. Here again, we have a literal fulfillment of a prophecy made, even by the date accepted for Daniel by critics, over 2,000 years in advance.

In view of the detailed, specific, and literal nature of these fulfilled predictions, they offer proof of the infallible foreknowledge of the God who inspired them. However, if neotheism is correct, these are not examples of infallible foreknowledge. Their remoteness from the events predicted and specificity rule out their being based on reading the trends of the times. The remaining supposition that only the predictions that were going to come to pass were put in the Bible is implausible, since it would take infallible foreknowledge to know which ones these would be. The only reasonable alternative is that the God who inspired these predictions has infallible foreknowledge of the future—a conclusion directly contrary to neotheism.

As noted above, repeated, specific, and unfailing predictions of events involving human free choice are evidence of infallibility. And the above predictions fit into that category. Thereby they lend strong support to the falsification of neotheism, which claims that God cannot make such predictions.

TWELVE OBJECTIONS TO A FINITE GOD

1. How can a finite (limited) God achieve a better world? The fixity of physical laws and the persistence of evil over the thousands of years of human history argues against this kind of God ever achieving a better world than the present one.
2. Given his limitations, why did this finite God who could not overcome evil engage in such a wasteful attempt as this world?
3. How can evil be absorbed into the nature of God? Isn't this strange, dualistic combination of good and evil in God inherently incoherent?
4. How can a finite God accomplish a better world by way of the cooperation of human beings when the vast majority of them seem almost totally unaware of his purposes?
5. How can a limited God who does not control the actual events of this world provide any real assurance that there will be a growth of value?
6. What value to present individuals is a promise of serial appearance of the maximal amount of value? This is like promising a million dollars to a family over the next 1,000 generations.
7. How could such a God be given "absolute admiration" (cf. Hartshorne) as retainer of all past value when: (a) This stored value is not experienced by any actual entity and (b) This is mere preservation without any assurance of progress?
8. How can a finite God be morally worthy who allows all the pain of this world in order to enrich his own aesthetic value? Is all this evil worth it merely for beauty's sake?
9. How can anyone worship a God who is so helpless that he not only does not control what happens in the world but he cannot

even "call the whole thing off"? Is not such a God so paralyzed as to be perilous?

10. How can a God who is identical with the world (in his actuality) be genuinely personal when he is identical with us?

11. How can a God be morally perfect when he is engaged in a self-character-building activity at our expense in his efforts to overcome evil?

12. How can one avoid making individual evil illusory by saying that victory over evil is really God's vicarious triumph in us?

Two observations are relevant to these criticisms. First, none of these objections really applies to a theistic God. In fact, a theistic God would be the answer to all of these objections. For example, an all-powerful, all-good, and all-knowing God can and will overcome evil without enriching himself at our expense. And as absolutely good and powerful, a theistic God is worthy of our worship and commitment (See *Roots of Evil* [Dallas, Tex.: Word Publishing Co., 1989], chap. 3). Second, many of these objections have some degree of applicability to the God of neotheism, since he too is limited in his knowledge, not knowing for sure how things will turn out.

These are adapted from the book *Evil and the Concept of God* by Edward H. Madden and P. H. Hare (Springfield, Ill.: Charles C. Thomas, 1968), chap. 6.

GLOSSARY

Actuality. That which is actual as opposed to that which merely has potentiality (see). Pure Actuality is the attribute of God that excludes all potentiality from him (see Aseity), including the possibility of nonexistence (see Necessary Being).

A priori. Prior to or independent of experience (as opposed to *a posteriori*).

A posteriori. From experience (as opposed to *a priori*).

Accidence (an accident). A nonessential attribute; something that is not necessary to a substance (see) but only inheres in it.

Agnosticism. The belief that one cannot or at least does not know reality, or especially, God.

Analogical. Similar; both the same and different as opposed to equivocal (totally different) and univocal (entirely the same).

Analogy. That which is similar as opposed to that which is identical or that which is totally different.

Antinomy. A logical contradition.

Apologetics. The discipline that deals with defending the Christian faith. From the Greek word *apologia* (defense) as in 1 Peter 3:15.

Aseity. Self-existence; the attribute of God that affirms he exists in and of himself, independent from anything else (see also Actuality).

Atheism. The worldview that affirms there is no God as opposed to theism (see), which asserts there is a God.

Being. Something that exists; what is real as opposed to non-being, which is nothing, or nonexistence.

Bipolar. Having two poles or dimensions (synonymous with dipolar). A view of God held by panentheism (see) or process theology.

Cause (efficient). That which brings about an effect; the agent, producer, or that by which something comes to be.

Contingent. Dependent on another; a contingent being (see) is dependent on another for its existence.

Cosmological Argument. An argument for God's existence that begins with the cosmos and concludes it must have a Creator; a posteriori (see) argument from effect to cause (see also Kalam Argument).

Deism. The belief in one infinite personal and transcendent God who created the world but does not intervene in it in a supernatural way; theism (see) minus miracles.

Demiurgos. Plato's view of God; a finite eternal Former of the world who forms the eternal chaos into a cosmos by eternal Forms that always existed in the Perfect Form (called the Good); an eternal but limited God who creates *ex materia* (see).

Determinism. The belief that everything is determined. Strong (hard) determinism denies that any acts are truly free (see Free Will). Soft determinism holds that events can be both determined (by God) and yet freely chosen by human beings.

Ex Deo. Literally "out of God"; the view of origins held by pantheism (see) and panentheism (see) that affirms God produced the world out of himself, that the world is part of God.

Ex materia. Literally, "out of matter"; the view of origins that asserts the universe has taken shape out of preexisting matter or stuff either by a Former (see Demiurgos) or by some natural process (as in Atheism).

Ex nihilo. Literally, "out of nothing"; the view of creation held by theism (see) that in the beginning God made something out of nothing as opposed to making it out of some eternal stuff (see *ex materia*) or out of himself (see *ex Deo*).

Epistemology. From the Greek *episteme*, to know; the study of knowledge; how we know.

Equivocal. Totally different as opposed to entirely the same (univocal) and similar (analogical).

Essence. The nature of something; *what* it is as opposed to *that* it is, its existence (see).

Existence. That which is; the actual; being; reality. *That* something is as opposed to *what* it is (essence).

Finite. Having limits or boundaries as opposed to being infinite (see).

Finite Godism. The belief that there is a God who made the world but who is limited in power and/or perfection, such as Plato's Demiurgos (see).

Free Will. The power of human beings to perform certain human actions that are free from external and/or internal constraint; the ability to cause certain actions by one's self without coercion from another (see Determinism).

Infinite. Literally, "not limited"; without boundaries or limitations.

Immanence. God's presence within the universe as compared with his transcendence (see) over it.

Immutability. The attribute of God that makes it impossible for him to change; God's unvariable nature.

Inerrancy. Without error; errorless (see Infallible).

Infallible. Literally, "not fallible or breakable"; a term used to describe the Bible's utter reliability (see Inerrancy).

Kalam Argument. A form of the cosmological argument (see) for God's existence whose starting point is that the universe has a beginning and, therefore, must have a Beginner (Cause).

Metaphysics. The study of being or reality as such (see Ontology).

Necessary Being. A Being that must exist; it *cannot* not exist (as opposed to a contingent (see) being which *can* not exist.

Neotheism. Literally "New Theism"; a modification of classical theism (see) in the direction of panentheism (see) or process theology; a form of theism (see) that denies God is simple, immutable, nontemporal, and fully omniscient.

Ontology. The study of being (from Greek *ontos*, being); synonymous with metaphysics (see).

Panentheism. The belief that all is in God as opposed to pantheism (see), which claims all is God; that God has two poles, that is, is bipolar (see); also called process theology (see).

Pantheism. The belief that all is God and God is all; God is identical to all that is; that "creation" is part of God, flowing from him *ex Deo* (see).

Polytheism. The belief that there are many finite gods (see), not just one finite god as in Finite Godism (see) or one Infinite God (see theism).

Potentiality. That which can be; the ability to be actualized (see Actuality).

Process Theology. The view that God is finite and constantly changing; also called panentheism (see) or bipolar (see) theism.

Relativism. The view that there are no absolutes; that all truth and/ or values are relative and changing.

Substance. The nature of something; that which is essential to a thing as opposed to an accidence (see); what it *is* by its nature in contrast to what it merely *has* but need not have.

Theism. The belief in one infinite personal transcendent and immanent God who created the world *ex nihilo* (see) and who also intervenes in it supernaturally on occasion.

Transcendence. That which is more or goes beyond; that fact of God's being beyond the universe and not only in it (see Immanence).

Univocal. Entirely the same as opposed to totally different (equivocal) or similar (analogical).

GENERAL
BIBLIOGRAPHY

Aquinas, Thomas. "The Summa Theologica," in *Basic Writings of Saint Thomas Aquinas.* Vol. 1. Edited and Annotated, with an Introduction by Anton C. Pegis. New York: Random House, 1944.

Basinger, David and Randall. "Inerrancy, Dictation, and the Free Will Defense." *The Evangelical Quarterly* 55:3 (July 1983): 177–180.

Basinger, David. *The Case for Freewill Theism.* Downers Grove, Ill.

Basinger, David, ed. *Predestination and Free Will.* Downers Grove, Ill.: InterVarsity, 1986.

Beckwith, Frank. "Limited Omniscience and the Test for a Prophet: A Brief Philosophical Analysis." *Journal of the Evangelical Theological Society* 36/3 (September 1993): 362.

Boyd, Greg. *Trinity and Process.* New York: Peter Lang, 1992.

Craig, William. *The Kalam Cosmological Argument.* London: The Macmillan Press, Ltd., 1979.

Davis, Stephen T. *Logic and the Nature of God.* Grand Rapids, Mich.: Eerdmans, 1983.

Ford, Lewis. "Biblical Recital and Process Philosophy." *Interpretation* (April 1972): 201.

———. *The Lure of God.* New York: U. Press of America, 1985.

Garrigou-Lagrange, Reginald. *God: His Existence and Nature.* St. Louis: B. Herder Book Co., 1946.

———. *Reality: A Synthesis of Thomistic Thought.* London: B. Herder Book Co., 1950.

Geach, Peter. *Providence and Evil.* Cambridge: University Press, 1977.

Geisler, Norman. *Christian Apologetics.* Grand Rapids, Mich.: Baker Books, 1976.

————. *Thomas Aquinas: An Evangelical Appraisal.* Grand Rapids, Mich.: Baker Books, 1991.

Geisler, Norman, ed. *Inerrancy.* Grand Rapids, Mich.: Zondervan Publishing Co., 1979.

Geisler, N. L., and Ron Brooks. *When Skeptics Ask.* Wheaton, Ill.: Victor Books, 1990.

Geisler, N. L., and Thomas Howe. *When Critics Ask.* Wheaton, Ill.: Victor Books, 1992.

Geisler, N. L., and William Watkins. *Worlds Apart.* Grand Rapids, Mich.: Baker Book House, 1989.

Gilson, Etienne. *God and Philosophy.* New Haven: Yale University Press, 1941.

Gruenler, Royce G. *The Inexhaustible God.* Grand Rapids, Mich.: Baker Book House, 1983.

Hartshorne, Charles. *Aquinas to Whitehead: Seven Centuries of Metaphysics of Religion.* Milwaukee: Marquette University Publications, 1976.

————. *Creative Synthesis and Philosophic Method.*

————. *The Divine Relativity: A Social Conception of God.* New Haven and London: Yale University Press, 1948.

————. "The Dipolar Conception of Deity." *The Review of Metaphysics* 21 (December 1967): 287.

————. *The Logic of Perfection.* LaSalle: The Open Court Publishing Company, 1962.

————. "Love and Dual Transcendence." *Union Seminary Quarterly Review* 30 (Winter-Summer 1975): 97.

————. *Man's Vision of God and the Logic of Theism.* Hamden: Archon Books, 1964.

————. *A Natural Theology for Our Time.* LaSalle: The Open Court Publishing Company, 1967.

Hasker, William. *God, Time, and Knowledge.* Ithaca: Cornell University Press, 1989.

Hick, John, ed. "Is God's Existence a State of Affairs?" in *Faith and Philosophy.* London: St. Martin's Press, 1966.

Hume, David. *Enquiry Concerning Human Understanding.* Indianapolis: Bobbs-Merrill, 1955.

Lucas, J. R. *The Freedom of the Will.* Oxford: Oxford University Press, 1970.

———. *The Future: An Essay on God, Temporality, and Truth.* London: Basil Blackwell, 1989.

Madden, Edward H., and P. H. Hare. *Evil and the Concept of God.* Springfield, Ill.: Charles C. Thomas, 1968.

Morris, Thomas V. *Our Idea of God: An Introduction to Philosophical Theology.* Downer's Grove, Ill.: InterVarsity, 1991.

Nash, Ronald, ed. *The Concept of God.* Grand Rapids, Mich.: Zondervan, 1983.

———. *Process Theology.* Grand Rapids, Mich.: Baker, 1987.

Ogden, Schubert. *The Reality of God and Other Essays.* San Francisco: Harper & Row, 1977.

———. "Toward a New Theism," in *Process Theology and Christian Thought,* ed., Delwin Brown, et al. Indianapolis: Bobbs-Merrill, 1971.

Pinnock, Clark. "Between Classical and Process Theism." *Process Theology,* ed., Ronald Nash. Grand Rapids, Mich.: Baker, 1987.

Ramm, Bernard. *Protestant Christian Evidences.* Chicago: Moody Press, 1953.

Rice, Richard. *God's Foreknowledge and Man's Free Will.* Minneapolis: Bethany House Publishers, 1985.

Smith, Joseph. *Teaching of the Prophet Joseph Smith,* 4th edition, ed., Joseph Fielding Smith. Salt Lake City: The Deseret News Press, 1943.

Swinburne, Richard. *The Coherence of Theism.* Oxford: University Press, 1977.

Whitehead, Alfred North. *Process and Reality.* New York: Harper Torchbooks, 1960.

Zagzebski, Linda. *The Dilemma of Freedom and Foreknowledge.* Oxford: Oxford University Press, 1991.

SELECT
BIBLIOGRAPHY

Anselm, St. *Proslogion.*

Aquinas, Thomas. *Summa Theologica* in *Basic Writings of Saint Thomas Aquinas.* Vol. 1. Edited and Annotated, with an Introduction by Anton C. Pegis. New York: Random House, 1944.

———. *Summa Contra Gentiles,* trans. by Vernon Bourke as *On the Truth of the Catholic Faith.* New York: Hanover House, 1956.

———. *Monologion.*

Augustine, St. *City of God.* Edited by Vernon Bourke. New York: Doubleday, 1958

———. *Confessions.*

———. *The Summa Contra Gentiles.*

Calvin, John. *Institutes of the Christian Religion.*

Charnock, Stephen. *Discourse Upon the Existence and Attributes of God.* Grand Rapids, Mich.: Baker Books, 1979 (1853 reprint).

Collins, James. *God and Modern Philosophers.* Chicago: Regnery, 1959.

Garrigou-Lagrange, Reginald. *God: His Existence and Nature.* St. Louis: B. Herder Book Co., 1946.

———. *Reality: A Synthesis of Thomistic Thought.* London: B. Herder Book Co., 1950.

———. *The Trinity and the Creator.* St. Louis: B. Herder Book Co., 1952.

———. *The One God.* St. Louis: B. Herder Book Co., 1943.

Geisler, Norman. *Christian Apologetics.* Grand Rapids, Mich.: Baker Books, 1976.

———. *Thomas Aquinas: An Evangelical Appraisal.* Grand Rapids, Mich.: Baker Books, 1991.

Geisler, N. L., and William Watkins. *Worlds Apart.* Grand Rapids,

Mich.: Baker Book House, 1989.

George P., et al. *Being and God.* New York: Appleton-Century-Crofts, 1963.

Gilson, Etienne. *God and Philosophy.* New Haven: Yale University Press, 1941.

Gruenler, Royce G. *The Inexhaustible God.* Grand Rapids, Mich.: Baker Book House, 1983.

Kreeft, Peter. *Summa of the Summa.*

Mascall, Eric L. *He Who Is.* London: Longmans, Green and Co., 1949.

Owen, H. P. *Concepts of Deity.* New York: Herder and Herder, 1971.

NOTES

Chapter 1

1. Harold Kushner, *When Bad Things Happen to Good People* (New York: Avon Books, Div. of Hearst Corp., 1983).
2. Harold Kushner, *How Good Do We Have to Be?* (Denver: Little Books, & Co., 1996).
3. See Joseph Smith, *Teaching of the Prophet Joseph Smith,* edited by Joseph Fielding Smith, 4th ed. (Salt Lake City: The Deseret News Press, 1943), pp. 349–532.
4. See William Watkins, *The New Absolutes* (Minneapolis: Bethany House Publishers, 1996).
5. Jean Paul Sartre, *Nausea* (New Directions, 1959), p. 57.
6. See N. L. Geisler, *When Skeptics Ask* (Grand Rapids, Mich.: Baker Books, 1996).
7. See N. L. Geisler, *Christian Apologetics* (Grand Rapids, Mich.: Baker Books, 1976).
8. See N. L. Geisler and William Watkins, *World's Apart* (Grand Rapids, Mich.: Baker Books, 1989).

Chapter 2

1. Thomas Aquinas, *Summa Theologica,* Vols. 1, 2, 3, Christian Classics, 1981.
2. Ibid., 1a. 9, 1.
3. Exodus 3:14.
4. Thomas Aquinas, *Summa Theologiae,* 1a. 9, 2, Christian Classics, 1991.
5. Ibid., 1a. 10, 1.
6. Ibid., 1a. 10, 2.
7. Ibid., 1a. 10, 3.
8. Ibid., 1a. 10, 4.
9. Ibid., Reply to Objection 2.

10. Ibid., 1a. 11, 3.
11. Ibid., 1a. 13, 7.
12. Ibid., 1a. 13, 7 ad 2.
13. Ibid., 1a. 13, 7 ad 5.
14. Ibid., 1a. 14, 2.
15. Ibid., 1a. 14, 3.
16. Ibid., 1a, 14, 10.
17. Ibid., 1a. 14, 4.
18. Ibid., 1a. 14, 5.
19. Ibid., 1a. 14, 15.
20. Ibid., 1a. 15, 2.
21. Ibid., 1a. 14, 11.
22. Ibid., 1a. 14, 6.
23. Ibid., 1a. 14, 7.
24. Ibid., 1a. 14, 7 ad 2.
25. Ibid., 1a. 14, 7 ad 3 and 4.
26. Ibid., 1a. 14, 8.
27. Ibid., 1a. 14, 8, ad 2.
28. Ibid., 1a. 14, 9.
29. Ibid., 1a. 14, 13.
30. Ibid., 1a 14, ??.
31. See N. L. Geisler in Basinger, *Free Will and Predestination* (Downer's Grove, Ill.: InterVarsity Press, 1986).
32. *Summa Theologiae*, 1a. 19, 1.
33. Ibid., 1a. 19, 2.
34. Ibid., 1a. 19, 2 ad 1.
35. Ibid., 1a. 19, 2 ad 2.
36. Ibid., 1a. 19, 2 ad 3.
37. Ibid., 1a. 19, 2 ad 4.
38. Ibid., 1a. 19, 3 ad 3.
39. Ibid., 1a. 19, 3.
40. Ibid., 1a. 19, 4.
41. Ibid., 1a. 19, 4 ad 1.
42. Ibid., 1a. 19, 5.
43. Ibid., 1a. 19, 6.
44. 2 Peter 3:9, KJV.
45. *Summa Theologiae*, 1a. 19, 6 ad 2.
46. Ibid., 1a. 19, 7.

Chapter 3

1. Schubert Ogden, *The Reality of God and other Essays* (San Francisco: Harper & Row, 1977), p. 61, cf. p. 176.

2. ———. "Toward a New Theism" in *Process Philosophy and Christian Thought,* ed. Delwin Brown, et al. (Indianapolis: Bobbs-Merrill, 1971) p. 186.
3. Charles Hartshorne, *The Logic of Perfection* (LaSalle: The Open Court Publishing Co., 1962), p. 126.
4. ———. *Man's Vision of God,* p. 348.
5. Ibid., p. 177.
6. Ibid., pp. 184–185.
7. Alfred North Whitehead, *Process and Reality,* p. 95.
8. Ibid., p. 122.
9. Charles Hartshorne, *Creative Synthesis and Philosophic Method,* pp. 13, 118.
10. ———. *Man's Vision of God and the Logic of Theism,* p. 211.
11. Whitehead, *Process and Reality,* p. 134.
12. Hartshorne, "The Bipolar Conception of Deity" in *The Review Metaphysics* 21 (December, 1967): p. 287.
13. ———. *A Natural Theology for Our Time,* pp. 76–77.
14. Ibid., p. 104.
15. Hartshorne, *The Logic of Perfection,* 35.
16. ———. *Creative Synthesis and Philosophic Method,* p. 249.
17. ———. *A Natural Theology for Our Time,* pp. 126–137.
18. ———. *Aquinas to Whitehead: Seven Centuries of Metaphysics of Religion* Marquette Press, 1976 p. 33.
19. ———. *A Natural Theology for Our Time,* p. 21.
20. ———. "Love and Dual Transcendence" in *Union Seminary Quarterly Review* 30 (Winter-Summer, 1975), p. 97.
21. ———. *Creative Synthesis and Philosophic Method,* p. 125.
22. ———. *The Divine Relativity,* p. 83.
23. Hartshorne, *Man's Vision of God,* p. 31.
24. Ibid., pp. 155–156.
25. Ibid., p. 111.
26. Hick, John, ed. "Is God's Existence a State of Affairs?" in *Faith and Philosophy* (London: St. Martin's Press, 1966), p. 30.
27. Lewis Ford, "Biblical Recital and Process Philosophy" in *Interpretation* (April 1972), p. 201.
28. See Lewis Ford, *The Lure of God,* New York: U. Press of America, 1985.
29. Hartshorne, *A Natural Theology for Our Time,* pp. 113–114.
30. Whitehead, *Process and Reality,* p. 169.
31. Ibid., p. 529.
32. Lewis Ford, "Biblical Recital and Process Philosophy" in *Interpretation* 26.2 (April 1972), p. 201.
33. Alfred North Whitehead, *Process and Reality,* p. 517.

34. Hartshorne, *The Logic of Perfection*, p. 14.
35. Ibid.
36. Ford, ibid., pp. 202–203.
37. Ogden, *Faith and Freedom*, pp. 76–77.
38. Thomas Aquinas, *Summa Theologica*, 1a.a.1.
39. Ogden, *The Reality of God*, pp. 18–19, 44.
40. Hartshorne, *Aquinas to Whitehead*, p. 33.
41. Charles Hartshorne, *Creative Synthesis and Philosophic Method* (LaSalle, Ill.: Open Court Publishers, 1970), p.48.
42. Ibid.
43. Molinism springs from the Spanish Jesuit theologian Luis de Molina (1535–1600), who argued that God had "middle knowledge" that was dependent on future free acts of human beings. This was strongly opposed by the Dominicans who argued that God's knowledge cannot be dependent on anything, since it is part of his being and God is a totally independent being (see Reginald Garrigou-Lagrange, *Reality: a Synthesis of Thomistic Thought* (London: B. Herder Book Co., 1950), pp. 107–131.
44. See N. L. Geisler and William Watkins, *Worlds Apart* (Grand Rapids, Mich.: Baker Book House, 1989), chap. 5.
45. Ogden, "The Reality of God," p. 47.
46. ———. "Toward a New Theism," in *Process Theology and Christian Thought*, p. 185.
47. *The Reality of God*, pp. 153–154.
48. Ibid., p. 155.
49. Ibid., pp. 122, 124.
50. Ogden, "Toward a New Theism," in *Process Philosophy and Christian Thought*, p. 186.
51. Hartshorne, *Aquinas to Whitehead*, pp. 22–24.
52. This is not the same, as some argue, as saying there must be infinitely tall persons because we know there are some persons taller than others. For "taller" deals with quantity, whereas better deals with quality. And unlike quantity where actual infinites are impossible, it is possible to have an infinitely perfect being (since there is no contradiction in the concept).
53. Royce G. Gruenler, *The Inexhaustible God* (Grand Rapids, Mich.: Baker Book House, 1983), p. 16.
54. Ibid., p. 20.
55. Ibid., p. 18.
56. Ibid., p. 20.
57. Ibid.
58. Ibid., p. 16.

59. Paul Tillich, *Ultimate Concern*, ed., D. Mackenzie Brown (London: SCM, 1965), pp. 43–46.
60. Schubert Ogden, "What Is Theology?" *Journal of Religion* 52, no. 1 (January 1972), p. 26.

Chapter 4

1. Clark Pinnock, "Between Classical and Process Theism" in *Process Theology*, Ronald Nash, ed. (Baker, 1987); William Hasker, *God, Time, and Knowledge* (Cornell University Press, 1989); David and Randall Basinger, eds., *Predestination and Free Will* (Inter Varsity, 1986); David Basinger, *The Case for Free Will Theism* (InterVarsity Press, 1996).

2. Those who have written books include Stephen T. Davis, *Logic and the Nature of God* (Grand Rapids: Eerdmans, 1983); Richard Rice, *God's Foreknowledge and Man's Free Will* (Bethany House, 1985); Ronald Nash, ed., *Process Theology* (Grand Rapids: Baker, 1987) and *The Concept of God* (Grand Rapids: Zondervan, 1983); Greg Boyd, *Trinity and Process* (New York: Peter Lang, 1992) and *Letters From a Skeptic* (Victor, 1994); J. R. Lucas, *The Freedom of the Will* (Oxford, 1970) and *The Future: an Essay on God, Temporality, and Truth* (London: Basil Blackwell, 1989); Peter Geach, *Providence and Evil* (Cambridge, 1977); Richard Swinburne, *The Coherence of Theism* (Oxford, 1977); Thomas V. Morris, *Our Idea of God: an Introduction to Philosophical Theology* (InterVarsity, 1991), is close to the view. And A. N. Prior, Richard Purtill, and others have written articles defending neotheism. Still others show sympathy to the view, such as Stephen T. Davis, *Logic and the Nature of God* (Eerdmans, 1983), and Linda Zagzebski, *The Dilemma of Freedom and Foreknowledge* (Oxford University Press, 1991).

3. Pinnock correctly positioned it in the title of his chapter "Between Classical and Process Theism" in *Process Theology*, Ronald Nash, ed. (Baker, 1987).

4. By a "libertarian" or "incompatiblist" view of free will they mean "an agent is free with respect to a given action at a given time if at that time it is within the agent's power to perform the action and also in the agent's power to refrain from the action" (pp. 136–137). This they distinguish from a compatiblist view by adding for the latter that the agent has this power *only if he chooses* to perform or not to perform the act. On a libertarian view one has both the "inner freedom" (no overwhelming desire to the contrary) and "outer freedom" to perform the act. On the compatiblist view, one need only have the "outer freedom" (i.e., be free from external restraints). On the libertarian view one must be free in both desire and decision, but on the compatiblist view one

need only be free to decide, not to desire or to do, the action.

5. See R. Alan Cole, *Exodus* (London: Tyndale Press, 1970), p. 69.

6. See the article on "YHWH" in *The Theological Dictionary of the Old Testament*, Vol. 5, p. 500 (emphasis added).

7. Arthur Preuss, *God: His Knowability, Essence, and Attributes* (St. Louis: B. Herder Book Co., 1930), p. 172.

8. Indeed, it would seem that the only sense in which God has what is nonessential to his nature is his acts. And classical theists readily admit that God engages in different and changing actions. But all of these flow from his unchanging nature as occasioned by the changing conditions in his creation (see chapters 5–6).

Chapter 5

1. All numbers cited in the text are from Clark Pinnock, et al., *The Openness of God* (InterVarsity, 1994).

2. See Etienne Gilson, *God and Philosophy* (New Haven: Yale University Press, 1941), chap. 1.

3. Ibid.

4. See William Craig, *The Kalam Cosmological Argument* (London: The Macmillan Press, Ltd., 1979).

5. See Thomas Aquinas, *The Summa Theologica*, Vols. 1, 2, 3, and Norman L. Geisler, *Christian Apologetics* (Grand Rapids, Mich.: Baker Book House, 1976), chap. 13.

6. For an infinite number of moments cannot be traversed before creation or else creation would never have come. But creation did occur (cf. Kalam Argument). Hence, God must have been nontemporal before creation. And whatever he knew (which is everything knowable according to neotheists), he must have known nontemporally.

7. See Norman L. Geisler, *Thomas Aquinas: an Evangelical Appraisal* (Grand Rapids, Mich.: Baker Books, 1991), chap. 10.

8. Aquinas, *Summa Theologica* 1a. 13, 7.

9. See William Hasker, *God, Time, and Knowledge* (Ithaca: Cornell University Press, 1989), p. 188.

10. *Summa Theologica*, 1a. 14, 4.

11. Ibid., 1a. 19, 7.

12. Of course, in one sense of the term, classical theists place "limitations" on God's foreknowledge, namely, he can only know what is possible to know. God cannot know what is contradictory (like square circles). But this is not really a limitation; it simply says he knows in an unlimited and consistent way, because his nature is both unlimited and consistent.

13. Aquinas, *Summa Theologiae*, 1a. 14, 9.

14. Ibid., 1a. 14, 13.
15. It is important to observe here that it is a category mistake to argue that the future does not yet exist and so it cannot yet exist in God's now. For the way it exists in God's now is not the same as the way it will exist in man's future. Again, God knows *what* we know but not the *way* we know it. The way the future exists for us is temporally. But the way it exists in God's knowledge is eternally.

Chapter 6

1. See William Craig, *The Kalam Cosmological Argument* (London: The Macmillan Press, Ltd., 1979).
2. David Hume, *Enquiry Concerning Human Understanding* (Indiana, Ind.: Bobbs-Merrill, 1955), pp. 165–166.
3. Process theology admits that God's potential (primordial) nature is indestructible, being made up of an infinite number of eternal objects (forms). But there are two problems with neotheism falling back on this kind of explanation. First, it would reduce their view to process theology, which they claim to reject. Second, even process theology does not solve the problem. For in God's actual nature he would still be destructible. He is only indestructible in his potential (primordial) nature. So, in either case God could actually be destroyed, that is, reduced to an infinite number of tiny little spiritual "atoms" or platonic-like forms. For classical theism this is not possible, since God is pure actuality and absolute simplicity with no potential for division or destruction.

Chapter 7

1. See Randy and David Basinger, "Inerrancy, Dictation, and the Free Will Defense" in *The Evangelical Quarterly* 55:3 (July 1983), pp. 177–180.
2. For further discussion on the inerrancy (errorlessness) of the Bible, see N. L. Geisler, ed., *Inerrancy* (Grand Rapids, Mich.: Zondervan Publishing Co., 1979). See also, Geisler, *When Critics Ask* (Grand Rapids, Mich.: Baker Book House, 1992), especially chap. 1.
3. Frank Beckwith, "Limited Omniscience and the Test for a Prophet: a Brief Philosophical Analysis" in *Journal of the Evangelical Theological Society 36/3* (September 1993), p. 362.
4. Bernard Ramm, *Protestant Christian Evidences* (Chicago: Moody Press, 1953), p. 81.
5. Payne, *Encyclopedia of Biblical Prophecy.* pp. 665–670.
6. see Harold Hoehner, *Chronological Aspects of the Life of Christ* (Grand Rapids, Mich.: Zondervan, 1978).

7. This is assuming that Daniel's 490 is not a round number, which is possible, since the Bible does use round numbers. In any event, even with a round number, Daniel's prediction takes us to the very time of Christ.
8. See R. Garrigou-LaGrange, *God: His Existence and Nature* (St. Louis: B. Herder Book Co., 1946), Appendix IV, pp. 465–528.

INDEX